MANAGED MONEY

The Experience of Sweden

A COUNTRY'S DEMAND IS NOT FOR A CERTAIN AMOUNT OF METALLIC [OR OTHER] CURRENCY; BUT FOR AN AMOUNT OF CURRENCY WHICH HAS A CERTAIN PURCHASING POWER.

ALFRED MARSHALL, "MONEY, CREDIT AND COMMERCE."

MANAGED MONEY

The Experience of Sweden

BY

ERIK T. H. KJELLSTROM

WITH A FOREWORD BY

H. PARKER WILLIS

PROFESSOR OF BANKING IN
COLUMBIA UNIVERSITY

NEW YORK · MCMXXXIV

MORNINGSIDE HEIGHTS

COLUMBIA UNIVERSITY PRESS

PUBLISHED 1934

PRINTED IN THE UNITED STATES OF AMERICA
THE CAYUGA PRESS · ITHACA, NEW YORK

TO

My Father

Foreword

Economists have never given to Sweden, or to Scandinavia generally, the attention that those countries deserve by reason of their long experience, their conservative standards, and their regard for their obligations. There has been a notable increase of recent years among British observers with respect to their interest in and attention to the Scandinavian states, and this growth has been particularly noticeable as concerns Sweden. American inquirers, on the other hand, had still maintained the attitude of neglect which had been so long characteristic, until, within the past two years or so, monetary and banking developments have become so urgent as to necessitate the search for information and new points of view in every country, no matter where situated, that offered real results of experimentation or theoretical inquiry.

Their attention once drawn to Swedish conditions, there has, as often happens, been some tendency on the part of those who had thus "discovered" Sweden to find unexpected demonstrations of their own preconceived ideas, and remarkable exemplifications of monetary doctrines which for unexplained reasons had failed to "work" elsewhere. Thus there has, of recent months, sprung up a superstition regarding Swedish "management" of money and banking, which has been widely advertised and exploited by academic and other adherents of the view that it was possible to move price levels about practically at will, by mere shifting of the quantity of credit "released" by a central bank, or by direction of the price level after other methods. The consequence has been the practice of dogmatically asserting, whenever exception was taken to some impossible or absurd application of monetary "management," that: "It works in Sweden, why not here?"—and as to this, inquirers into the truth have found a dearth of adequate material available for their study. Swedish economists, although often writing in languages other than their own, naturally devote themselves chiefly to facts as they observe them locally and write primarily for their own readers. Thus a considerable degree of explanation and interpretation is necessary if their data and conclusions are to be made really applicable to conditions prevailing elsewhere.

There was evidently a plain need for some careful study of the monetary policy and methods of the Bank of Sweden—the institution whose name has of recent months been so often taken in vain, and to which have been ascribed, by hasty exponents of "managed currency" ideas, such miraculous accomplishments in the way of foreign trade development, price control, and "stabilization" generally. Such a study is now afforded by Mr. Erik T. H. Kjellstrom. His study is written from the point of view of Sweden and with sympathy for and knowledge of conditions existing in that country. It is, moreover, written with full knowledge of the current bibliographical data available in the Swedish language, which is Mr. Kjellstrom's own. But it is also written on the basis of Mr. Kjellstrom's years of work in the United States, and his close examination of the American monetary and banking scene. Observation of the American conditions has enabled him to select those elements of Swedish experience most likely to be informative to students of money and banking on this side of the Atlantic, and to draw from them the conclusions and lessons that are most applicable to the situation that presents itself here. His book is thus a valuable sedative for the excited minds which are now evolving new and strange monetary theories which they (on hearsay) ascribe to Sweden as the originating source of experimentation.

Among the many elements in Swedish experience which Mr. Kjellstrom has chosen for analysis, those which will stand out as of conspicuous interest from the standpoint of the American reader relate to the movement of prices and production, to the credit policy of the Bank of Sweden, and to the foreign exchange and foreign trade phenomena with which the institution has had to deal. His conclusions nowhere pretend to develop new and striking discoveries; and will be the more confidently and positively received, in consequence, by American students. The author finds that in Sweden —as indeed in the United States—it is out of the question to trace any close dependence of actual events upon the policies of the central bank. He refuses completely to accept the prevailing superstition of a central bank as earthly providence. Further, says Mr. Kjellstrom, Sweden's abandonment of the gold standard and the depreciation of the krona abroad has not brought much advance in domestic wholesale prices, while it has proven impossible to "pump out" credit into the "market" —the effort so often and so vainly made by Federal Reserve banks in the endeavor to carry out what some of their directors have referred to as the "discoveries" they have made in the field of banking policy. Finally, as this monograph shows, the movements of import and export prices have been controlled much more largely by foreign market developments than by conditions within Sweden. "The monetary program has not been an adequate means to lift the country out of the grip of the depression."

Mr. Kjellstrom's volume is not only interesting in itself but is published at a time when it should have a wholesome and informative influence in American monetary discussion.

H. PARKER WILLIS

COLUMBIA UNIVERSITY
IN THE CITY OF NEW YORK
FEBRUARY 21, 1934

Preface

This book is offered to the public in the hope that it will help to explain to the layman the monetary program of the Bank of Sweden, which for some time has attracted a great deal of interest in this country. I have attempted to set forth the principal factors as they are disclosed in banking reports and in other publications. Any attempt to analyze the policies of a central bank meets with extreme difficulties, however, as much of the desired information is never made available to the public. This fact has made it hazardous to draw definite conclusions; whatever conclusions I have formulated are based, to the best of my knowledge, on reliable data.

In preparing the manuscript I have received valuable aid from Professors Benjamin H. Beckhart and John M. Chapman of the School of Business of Columbia University. I wish to take this opportunity to thank them for the assistance they have rendered me. I also want to thank Mr. Vladimir Kazakévich and Mr. Fritz Schumacher for their painstaking criticism.

E. T. H. K.

COLUMBIA UNIVERSITY
IN THE CITY OF NEW YORK
JANUARY, 1934

Contents

Tables and Charts

TABLES

CHARTS

Managed Money

CHAPTER I

INTRODUCTION

Managed money is by no means a new invention. Over a century ago—more specifically, in 1821—Sweden employed managed money to avert distortions of her price structure. Yet today the words "managed money" and "managed currency" seem to carry a connotation of novelty, and at times one of an almost magic formula, by means of which the purchasing power of money can be kept constant or changed at the discretion of the manager. Indeed, some of the believers in "a new money era" go so far as to say that money and credit are the sole determinants of prices, while still others are firmly convinced that even the most heterogeneous price structure can be raised or lowered to a uniform and consistent level merely by setting an arbitrary price for gold. Even if these enthusiasts disagree among themselves regarding some of the more subtle principles, they still seem to have one belief in common; that price stabilization is a sufficient means to initiate and later to preserve economic prosperity.

We are, no doubt, at present passing through one of the most bewildering periods in the history of business and finance. Conditions are chaotic. The old measure of values—money—no longer seems to serve its traditional purpose; and it is perhaps only natural that we are all looking for a stable yardstick with which to measure our gains and losses. Innumerable instruments have been suggested for this purpose, some of them sound, others unsound; but few of them have received serious attention, and still fewer have found their way into the monetary programs of governments.

Since the widespread departure from the gold standard, many countries have taken steps to "manage" their currencies. The objectives and methods vary widely. In the United States the Administration has declared its intention to obtain a dollar with unchanged purchasing power, not merely over a short period of time, but for the next generation as well. The devaluation of the dollar in terms of gold is regarded as a first step toward a "managed money."

For centuries man has dealt with money in one form or another, yet the problem of money and prices remains nearly as puzzling as ever. Indeed, the very concept of money as such is still clouded by a haze of contradictory beliefs and convictions. It is not the object here, however, to add to the denseness of this haze; rather, it is my purpose to present in simple terms the progress of Sweden's monetary program, in reference to which the *Monthly Review* of the Midland Bank of England for October-November 1932, says:

> It would be difficult to find an instance of a policy in monetary affairs more closely adapted to local conditions or more carefully and explicitly defined than that of Sweden, which left the gold standard only a few days after Great Britain.

Both in the United States and abroad the Swedish "managed currency" program has been heralded by many as a success, as an example for other governments to follow, and as a tribute to national homogeneity. Whatever we write or say about Sweden's monetary policy, no worthwhile appraisal of the program can be achieved without some knowledge of local conditions, the foundation upon which it rests, for it remains true that monetary policies must always be based upon the inherent traits of people, their banking habits, and the nature of their trade. A policy successful in one country cannot indiscriminately be imposed upon another nation, but some of the *fundamental* principles may well be applied elsewhere, always provided that the transplantation is intelligent.

CHAPTER II

The Swedish Background

There is somewhat of an air of solidity about the average Swedish person, and those who had the opportunity of following at close range the unfortunate and devastating disclosures of the unforgettable Kreuger crisis could not but admire the sobriety of this Scandinavian people. Then, in the midst of crashing fortunes and financial bewilderment, the Swedish public remained calm, collected, but intelligently interested. No runs on the banks occurred, not even on the institution most intricately enmeshed in Kreuger's financial spider web. The government acted swiftly and with a definiteness that caused widespread commendation at home and abroad. In the hastily summoned Parliament, socialists, liberals, and conservatives alike voiced their approval of the action of the Crown. Political affiliations and party dogmas were openly disavowed. The nation was in danger. It was a struggle to be waged by the entire nation, not one to be placed upon the shoulders of one or the other political party.

It is this high-minded spirit of social and civic coöperation which some observers believe to be responsible, in no small measure, for whatever success the government's present monetary program has had. Such a contention is no doubt open to criticism, particularly in view of the fact that for more than a year during the term of the monetary experiment Sweden has suffered from widespread strikes in two of her major industries. Still, the recognized homogeneity of the Swedish population has served as a good foundation for the monetary policies of the Bank of Sweden.

ECONOMISTS ARE INFLUENTIAL IN SWEDEN

The science and art of economics has long intrigued the Swedish mind, and few nations can point with more pride to an internationally recognized group of economic thinkers. The economists take an active part in the solution of the nation's economic problems. They do not hide their knowledge under the cloak of purely academic interests. The reputed stability and sound economic progress of the country is not a mere coincidence, and although much credit must be given to the sobriety of the public in general, the work and efforts of the nation's economists should not be minimized.

At present the Social Democratic Party controls the national government, and socialism enjoys a large following in Sweden. Some of the most important industries are state-owned or state-controlled. Nevertheless, highly "capitalistic" enterprises seem to find little difficulty in adjusting themselves to the Swedish brand of socialism.[1]

[1] See M. W. Childs, "Sweden: Where Capitalism Is Controlled," *Harper's Magazine*, No. 1002 (November, 1933), pp. 749-58.

SWEDEN'S STABLE BANKING SYSTEM

Sweden has, in many respects, been a pioneer in world social and economic developments. In the field of banking the nation introduced at an early date a system of currency and credit which only years later became widely accepted in other lands. Nevertheless, it is characteristic of Sweden that her banking history has not followed an unbroken path. Instead, it has evolved spasmodically. Carefully planned policies, after working for some time with fair success, have often been subjected to interference from the Crown, only to be tried again in the course of evolution, and finally adopted, this time with state approval.

On November 30, 1656, the town of Marienburg, in Prussia, witnessed the signing of the royal octroi for the first Swedish bank. The charter was granted to a certain John Palmstruch and his associates. The banks of Amsterdam, and also to some extent the banks of Hamburg, served as models for the "Palmstruchska Bank" which was the forerunner of the present "Riksbank," the Bank of Sweden. It is worthy of note that by the terms of the octroi the bank was given permission to open offices, not merely in Stockholm but in several other towns as well. It may be said, therefore, that branch banking was born with the Swedish banking system. The system of branch banking is, today, highly developed and it is possible—to use the British term—to talk of the "Big Four" of Sweden. Four banks are responsible for the major part of the nation's commercial banking activities[2] and it is most important to recognize that the Swedish banks are usually called upon not only to supply the working capital of industrial enterprises, but also to finance their long-term capital needs as well.[3]

The savings banks, it should be noted, play a more important rôle as competitors with the commercial banks than is the case in some other countries. Generally speaking, they are conservatively managed institutions; but the competition for deposits existing between them and the commercial institutions is at times a cause of difficulties, particularly in the event that the savings banks do not immediately adjust their interest rates to the changes in the official bank rate, as is the custom of the commercial banks.

Regarding the deposit business of the Swedish banks, Dr. Karin Kock in her *A Study of Interest Rates* remarks,

> two facts must be kept in mind. First, small investors are, as a rule, not accustomed to invest their capital directly in undertakings in the form of shares or bonds, but prefer to place their money as time deposits with the commercial banks or the savings banks. The banks have, therefore, founded their business on a great proportion of time deposits to demand deposits: at the end of 1927 time deposits including savings accounts, amounted to about 80 per cent of total deposits. Demand deposits consist of the ordinary current account (checkräkning) against which checks may be drawn, and

[2] In January 1934, a committee of experts was called to investigate the need for a state-owned commercial bank, as a means of facilitating long-term commercial credit for average sized enterprises.

[3] The Banking regulations prohibit banks from granting credits for more than one year. Loans are, however, renewed and may thus run for many years. Cf. Kock, *A Study of Interest Rates*, 235.

TABLE I

NUMBER OF OFFICES AND SUM TOTAL OF THE DEPOSITS IN COMMERCIAL AND SAVINGS BANKS[4]

	At the turn of the years							
	1900–01	1910–11	1913–14	1915–16	1917–18	1919–20	1925–26	1930–31
	Number of offices[1]							
Commercial banks (main offices and branches)	311	625	674	758	1,058	1,420	1,083[3]	1,070
Savings banks	745	952	888	891	1,010	1,324	1,309	1,087
	Number of offices per 100,000 inhabitants							
Commercial banks (main offices and branches)	6.1	11.3	12.0	13.3	18.2	24.3	17.9[3]	17.4
Savings banks	14.5	15.4	15.7	15.6	17.4	22.6	21.6	17.7
	Deposits[2] *in million kronor*							
Commercial banks (main offices and branches)	639	1,262	1,465	1,631	2,377	3,626	2,794	2,950
Savings banks	437	809	935	1,065	1,382	1,871	2,489	2,961
	Deposits in kronor per head							
Commercial banks (main offices and branches)	125	229	260	286	410	620	462	480
Savings banks	85	146	169	186	238	320	411	482

[1] Sources: "Svenska Bankplatser," issued by the Swedish Banks' Association; an article in "Ekonomisk Tidskrift" by C. H. Sjostedt, entitled "Några statistiska uppgifter angaende de svenska bankkontoren vid utgången av år 1900"; the official statistics regarding savings banks. [2] The term "deposits" does not include current account. [3] June 1926.

[4] The Skandinaviska Kreditaktiebolaget, *Quarterly Report*.

the special account with fourteen days' notice (uppsägningsräkning) which account is especially intended for business men who can thus invest temporary balances at a better rate of interest than can be earned on current account. This leads us to the other factor of importance to the deposit business of the banks, namely, the non-existence of an open money market. The business man, who has a temporary surplus which he wants to place in an interest-earning investment, has not the same opportunities to do so as have his colleagues in England and the United States. There is no bill market to which he may have recourse, and so he can only deposit his money with a bank. In recent years the practice of buying bonds for purposes of investments of balances has grown up, but the banks are still the receptacles into which the bulk of such funds flows. This has led to the creation of the special account mentioned above, and to the use by business undertakings of time deposits as investments for longer periods.

The bank note is of much greater importance as a means of payment in Sweden than in the United States. The use of checks is not nearly so widespread as in America, partly because the people are accustomed to the notes, and partly because of the use of "post bills": i.e., sight drafts which are drawn by a bank on its office or clearing agent in Stockholm. These "post bills" are payable without any deduction whatever at any bank office throughout Sweden. Such bills are widely used for remittances between different localities. The consequence, according to Dr. Kock, is that changes in the note circulation are of great primary interest, and that the best indicator of the position of the Bank of Sweden is the note reserve: i. e., the difference between the maximum limit of the note issue and the amount in circulation.

As this book is not directly concerned with the mechanism of Sweden's banking it is necessary to relate only a few more characteristic features of the banking organization before more detailed considerations of the position and methods of influence of the central institution are discussed. It may be of interest to point out that the banks generally take an active part in new bond issues, serving both as issue houses and underwriters. As a rule, they take up the whole issue and relieve the borrower from the risk of the market's failing to absorb the bonds. Only the government and municipalities have in a few instances tried to float loans without the banks acting as intermediaries. Some mortgage banks have in this respect, says Dr. Kock, a unique position: they issue their bonds by delivering to the borrowers the proceeds of the mortgage loan in bonds which the borrowers have then to dispose of in the market, or which the bank undertakes to sell for their account.

It might also be of interest to the American reader to note that the banks usually carry a very small volume of stocks in their own portfolios. The banking regulations impose heavy restrictions on the banks' ownership of stock, and they are, therefore, not in a position to take as active a part in underwriting stocks as they customarily do for bonds. Affiliated companies were introduced[6] to care for stock underwriting, but these companies soon discovered that they had had no experience in this field, and many of them subsequently failed. Except for the collapse of these affiliated companies and of some badly managed savings banks, bank failures are quite un-

[6] After the World War.

known in Sweden; one might indeed say that they are unknown.

The Stockholm Stock Exchange is the only institution of its kind in Sweden. Unlike the corresponding institutions in the United States, all the big banks in Sweden are members of the stock exchange. In dealing in stocks the banks act mainly as brokers, but in the bond market they buy and sell on their own account. Transactions in bonds are, however, to a great extent carried on outside the stock exchange. All transactions on the stock exchange are conducted on a cash basis, as the securities have to be physically delivered on the second day after the sale. As no organized system for "borrowing" stocks exists, bear operations are very rare.[6]

"THE BANK OF PARLIAMENT"

The Bank of Sweden holds a rather unique place among the world's central banking institutions. It is a bank of Parliament, a state institution, over which Parliament has direct supervision, while the Crown (King and Ministers) has no influence in the management of the Bank. The Crown appoints however, one member of the Board of Governors—the chairman—whose official duty it is to see that no single group or interest exercises undue influence upon the policies of the institution. Its designation as a bank of Parliament does not, however, imply that the Bank acts merely upon advice from Parliament. On the contrary, its independence and free-

[6] Kock, *op. cit.*., p. 238.

dom of action is guarded jealously both by Parliament itself and by the Board of Governors, although the Bank is responsible to the legislative branch of the government. With the reorganization of the old Palmstruchska Bank in 1668, Sweden was granted her first state bank, then a commercial institution, which dealt directly with the public. At present, however, a very small percentage of its loans and discounts are made on private customers' accounts.

With the modifications of the banking law of 1897, the Bank of Sweden became the sole note-issuing institution in the country, performing duties typical of a banker's bank. The Bank has still the right to carry on purely commercial functions; but it rarely accepts deposits from the general public. Its principal concern is now with the ordinary problems of a central bank. It has the authority to issue notes up to double the amount of its gold reserve and, in addition, 125 millions of kronor (one "krona" corresponds to 26.799 cents at mint par of exchange). However, in case of war or serious monetary disturbances, it is permitted to increase the fiduciary note issue by an additional 125 millions of kronor. The amount of the note issue not covered by gold must be backed by gilt-edged domestic bonds, foreign government bonds, gold deposited abroad or in transit, domestic or foreign bills of exchange, credit balances with some bank or accepting house abroad maturing within six months, and loans against gilt-edged domestic bonds or/and foreign government bonds.

The deposits of the Bank of Sweden consist merely (with few exceptions) of bankers' balances and government non-interest bearing deposits, the latter constituting the bulk of the Bank's deposit accounts. Normally, the banks hold very low balances with the central institution, limiting themselves to what is needed to meet the demands made on them in the clearing house. Such demands are made through the Bank of Sweden.

The commercial banks are normally indebted to the Bank of Sweden. The difference between the loans and discounts of the commercial banks and their own resources is *normally* (not merely temporarily) filled by the Bank of Sweden. Thus changes in the official bank rate affect the commercial banks *directly*. "Open market operations" (buying and selling of government securities) are seldom undertaken by the Bank, and the rediscount rate is, therefore, the Bank's foremost weapon.

Transactions in foreign exchange serve as a substitute, at least in part, for "open market operations." The commercial banks do not as a rule hold foreign balances in larger amounts than is needed for their ordinary business. If they have a surplus of foreign exchange they sell it to importers (or others) or to the Bank of Sweden. If the contrary is the case they buy foreign exchange from the Bank of Sweden. Their proceeds of their sales of foreign exchange to the Bank of Sweden is employed by the commercial banks as a basis for credit expansion or simply to reduce their indebtedness. A representative of the Bank of Sweden participates in the daily meeting of the commercial banks for the purpose of setting the official foreign exchange rates. It is understood that the Bank of Sweden has a great deal of influence at these meetings. The trend of the exchange rates, the levels of interest rates abroad as compared with the Bank's discount rate, as well as other factors of importance to the individual banks, normally determine the preference of the commercial banks for selling foreign exchange to the central bank or for rediscounting.[7] During the present monetary program transactions in the foreign exchange market have been of considerable importance because of the significance of foreign trade in Sweden's national economy.

SWEDEN'S EXTENSIVE FOREIGN TRADE

Sweden's industries have in no small measure developed from her foreign trade. In her national economy foreign trade plays a much more important rôle than is the case in many other countries. As regards both the volume and the value of foreign trade per capita, few countries in Europe can compare with Sweden. The underlying reason for the importance of her foreign trade is to be found mainly in Sweden's resources of raw materials and in her climatic conditions, which make possible a substantial excess production of some types of goods. Certain kinds of goods it is impossible to produce there, and yet Sweden is not to any great extent dependent on foreign markets for her foodstuffs; indeed, she is nearly self-supporting in this respect.

[7] Cf. Kock, *op. cit.*, pp. 188-89.

Sweden's exports have more than doubled since the World War. Nevertheless, her contribution to the world's trade, regarded in the aggregate, is still of quite modest proportions. About one and a half per cent of the world's total trade passes through the borders of Sweden. In spite of this small percentage, Sweden, in certain fields of foreign trade, contributes substantially to the world economy. This is especially true in regard to exports. Sweden supplies about 50 per cent of the iron ore that is sold in the world markets. Sweden also exports large quantities of chemical and mechanical wood pulp, and high grade steel. Swedish timber is, likewise, an important item in world trade.

Although Sweden has been somewhat favored as regards tariffs, largely because of the nature of her exports, which are mainly raw materials and semi-manufactured goods, some Swedish industries have, nevertheless, found it necessary to erect plants in foreign countries. This is particularly true of such industries as produce goods of superior quality. Obviously, this is also a form of export, which, however, does not figure in the statistics of Sweden's foreign trade. It may, therefore, be said that Sweden's export trade during the post-war period has been somewhat more advanced than is borne out by the actual trade statistics.

Although Sweden's consumption of the main staple commodities sold in the world market cannot normally compare with her exports of raw products and semi-manufactured goods, it was, nevertheless, the relatively high value of her im-

TABLE II

SWEDEN'S FOREIGN TRADE 1927-1932[8]

(In million kronor)

YEAR	IMPORTS	EXPORTS	IMPORT (−) OR EXPORT (+) TRADE SURPLUS	TOTAL TRADE
1927	1,584.4	1,616.6	+ 32.2	3,201.0
1928	1,708.0	1,574.7	−133.3	3,282.7
1929	1,782.6	1,812.3	+ 29.7	3,594.9
1930	1,662.2	1,550.4	−111.8	3,212.6
1931	1,427.5	1,122.4	−305.1	2,549.9
1932	1,147.9	944.8	−203.1	2,092.7

[8] Source: The Skandinavska Kreditaktiebolaget, *Quarterly Report*, April, 1933.

ports which was largely responsible for Sweden's abandonment of the gold standard.

While about 75 to 80 per cent of Sweden's imports, during the last few years, have come from the European continent, her trade with over-sea countries has been of increasing importance since the development of Swedish shipping. The European countries with which Sweden has the most important commercial relations are Great Britain and Germany; the United States dominates among the over-sea countries.

CHAPTER III

Sweden Forced Off Gold

Any attempt to analyze the Swedish monetary program would be quite difficult if one did not first give some consideration to the economic circumstances that compelled Sweden to abandon the gold standard. There is little doubt that the world economic depression was the ultimate cause of the widespread departure from gold which took place during the autumn of 1931, but as it would be impracticable, if not impossible, to trace the course of the world depression from its somewhat indefinite origin, we shall confine this part of our discussion to a chronological analysis of the more recent developments that caused Sweden to divorce her currency from gold.[1] A discussion of this type is necessary in order to draw attention to the economic factors that brought about the change in the monetary standard, as the same factors continued to influence events in Sweden after the currency was detached from gold.

It has often been pointed out that Sweden escaped from the effects of the depression longer than did many other countries. This is only partly true,

[1] Cf. Bankoutskottets Memorial No. 1, 1932; Karin Kock, "Hur Sverige Tvingades Att Överge Guldmyntfoten," appendix to Gunnar Myrdal, *Sveriges Väg Genom Penningkrisen*, and Skandinaviska Kreditaktiebolaget, Quarterly Reports, October, 1931, and January, 1932.

as the export industries had, during the latter part of 1930, already begun to restrict output, while home production was maintained fairly well. Since the purchasing power of the public showed only slight tendencies to decline, and since the standard of living was maintained at a relatively high level, the imports of goods for purposes of direct consumption and also for the requirements of home industries were considerable.

Importations were further facilitated by the circumstance that the Swedish price level was somewhat higher than the level of prices in the world markets. Another factor contributing to import trade was a considerable influx of long-term foreign capital and short-term funds deposited with the Swedish banks on foreign accounts. This led to a plethora of foreign exchange available for financing imports to Sweden. The relatively high purchasing value of Swedish currency in the international markets, which for several years had been a noteworthy circumstance, added further stimulus to import trade.

Moreover, as exports suffered from the general decline in prices abroad and from the decreased purchasing power in many foreign countries, it is easily understandable why Sweden's international exchange of goods during 1930 resulted in an excess of imports over exports of 114 million kronor, although the exchange of "invisible" items gave an excess of exports of 214 million kronor.

The following table shows Sweden's balance of international payments in the years 1928 to 1932, and gives a general picture of the development of

Sweden's international economic relations. In an article discussing Sweden's monetary policies[3] Professor David Davidson, of the University of Upsala, stresses the German price-reducing policies and the maldistribution of gold as two of the major reasons for the suspension of the gold standard in Sweden. After a highly interesting analysis Professor Davidson arrives at the conclusion that it was necessary for Sweden to divorce the krona from gold, and that this action ought to have been taken voluntarily had not trade and financial developments forced Sweden to abandon the gold standard.

It is necessary for our purpose, however, to omit a further discussion of Professor Davidson's analysis and center our attention on those facts and figures that ultimately compelled the government to follow the example of Great Britain.

HEAVY CAPITAL MOVEMENT DURING 1930

Sweden's import surplus of 114 millions of kronor in 1930 was more than covered by the invisible items, leaving approximately a hundred millions for investment abroad. The item "Transfers of capital" shows, however, that Sweden actually exported capital for long terms to an amount more than treble this figure, or about 342 million kronor. The reason for this is to be found in an influx of foreign capital to the Swedish commercial banks. This influx of short-term foreign capital into Sweden led to a plethora of foreign exchange in the Stockholm market, and it was

[3] *Ekonomisk Tidskrift*, 1932.

TABLE III

BALANCE OF INTERNATIONAL PAYMENTS 1928-1932[2]

(*In millions of kronor*)

	1928[1]	1929	1930	1931	1932
GOODS					
Exports	+1,575[1]	+1,813	+1,550	+1,135	+ 950
Imports	−1,708	−1,772	−1,664	−1,439	−1,166
Balance of trade	−133[1]	+ 41	−114	−304	−207
VARIOUS INVISIBLE ITEMS					
Freight receipts after deducting expenditure for coal, oil, etc., in foreign ports	+183	+205	+189	+139	+139
Remittances of Swedish Americans to home country	+ 35	+ 35	+ 30	+ 26	+ 35
Income (inclusive of profits) from Swedish capital abroad	+ 60	+110	+125	+108	+168
Interest and dividends on Swedish securities abroad	− 30	− 75	− 90	− 94	− 30
Interest paid to foreign countries on foreign holdings in Sweden	− 5	− 5	− 15	− 4[2]	0[2]
Expenditure of Swedish travelers abroad (after deducting expenditures of foreign travelers in Sweden) etc.	− 28	− 30	− 25	+ 2	+ 4
Total of various invisible items (net)	+215	+240	+214	+177	+316

TABLE III (continued)

BALANCE OF INTERNATIONAL PAYMENTS 1928-1932

(In millions of kronor)

	1928[1]	1929	1930	1931	1932
NET TOTAL OF GOODS AND VARIOUS INVISIBLE ITEMS	+ 82	+281	+100	−127	+109
TRANSFERS OF CAPITAL					
Sale to foreign countries of Swedish securities	+ 84	+130	+124	+149	+ 65
Sale to foreign countries of foreign securities	+ 41	+ 38	+ 74	+194	+154
Other, non-specified, influx of capital	+ 67	+ 90	+ 20	+448	+131
Repurchase of Swedish securities	− 56	− 95	−130	−128	− 49
Purchase of foreign securities	−134	−112	−405	−120	− 66
Other, non-specified, efflux of capital	−185	− 80	− 25	−491	−358
Total transfers of capital (net)	−183	− 29	−342	+ 52	−123
Gold, silver and coin (net)	− 13	− 15	− 3	+ 38[3]	+ 7[3]
Allowance for incomplete or doubtful data	+114	−237	+245	+ 37	+ 7

[1] In 1928 there were lengthy stoppages of work in some of Sweden's principal export industries.
[2] Inclusive of remittances to distressed persons in exbelligerent countries. [3] Only gold and gold coins.

[a] Source: The Skandinavska Kreditaktiebolaget.

particularly the Bank of Sweden that benefited from these short-term money movements. Part of the funds, thus obtained, were used for the financing of commodity imports, but also for the financing of long-term capital exports: i. e., imports of securities. No efforts seem to have been made at this time to halt this influx of "flight" capital, and at the end of the year foreign claims and obligations in Sweden totalled no less than four hundred millions of kronor. The reason for this influx is largely to be found in the circumstance that foreigners generally regarded Sweden as a sure haven for funds seeking fixed values. It was particularly during the spring of 1930 that the Swedish commercial banks became the receptacles of large volumes of short-term foreign funds. Normally, such an influx would not have been a cause of difficulties to the Swedish banking system. As it happened, however, that the Swedish banks employed the superabundance of foreign exchange as a basis for long-term capital exports, a foundation was laid for severe monetary disturbances in the event that the confidence crisis, visible already during 1930, should induce a withdrawal of these funds from the Swedish banks. It is, of course, always dangerous to employ short-term funds for long-term investments, but in this case, Sweden made what subsequent events proved to be a serious error of judgment.

CONTINUATION OF EXCESSIVE IMPORTS

The excess of commodity imports over exports continued unabated in the following year. During

1930 the excess had been 114 million kronor, while for the entire year 1931 the surplus of imports measured no less than 304 million kronor. Furthermore, during the first nine months of 1931 imports exceeded exports by 254 million kronor, or approximately three times the amount of the same period in 1930. As, furthermore, the excess of exports of invisible items diminished as compared to 1930,[4] the deficit in the balance of trade could be covered only by releasing Swedish claims abroad or by utilizing the inflow of foreign short-term capital as a means to pay for the surplus of commodity imports.

The superabundance of foreign exchange on the Swedish market also seems to have veiled the need for a thoroughgoing adjustment of wages and other elements of costs. No such adjustment was undertaken. As, furthermore, no tariff restrictions were imposed,[5] the decline in prices abroad, which to a great extent occurred in such commodity groups that comprise Sweden's import trade, caused a severe decline in import prices. This decline aggravated the distortion of the price structure. True, all wholesale price indices were declining at this time, but it is a noteworthy fact that neither export prices nor domestic prices fell to the same extent as did import prices. Sweden encountered, therefore, a shift in the structure of prices which also did not fail to influence demand, thereby

[4] See Table III.

[5] Tariff restrictions against those countries which for some time had carried on so-called foreign exchange dumping might have been defensible, but a general increase in tariffs could hardly have led to anything but foreign retaliations and consequent aggravation of domestic conditions.

aggravating the disequilibrium in the balance of trade, accentuated by mounting obstacles to Sweden's export trade. Indeed, Sweden suffered from having more favorable economic conditions than most other countries!

It is, of course, nothing unusual for a country to pay for an excess of imports by capital imports, but it should not be overlooked that, at this time, Sweden also imported a great deal of foreign securities. As, furthermore, the Kreuger concern could no longer obtain funds abroad, but had to borrow from the Swedish banks in order to obtain foreign exchange for payments abroad, the Governors of the Bank of Sweden found it necessary to suggest to the commercial banks that they reduce their imports of foreign securities. The Governors realized that a continuation of this process sooner or later was bound to endanger the liquidity of the banking system, particularly in view of the fact that the foreign deposits could be withdrawn, at any time, from the Swedish banks.

Already on February 6 the Bank of Sweden took steps to prevent a further influx of foreign short-term capital by lowering the official bank rate from three and a half to three per cent. This was not sufficient to stem the tide, however, and from the end of February to the end of May the commercial banks received no less than 105 million kronor of deposits on foreign banks' account. The total sum was then 343 million kronor, to which must be added substantial sums on private accounts.

THE EFFECT OF THE CENTRAL EUROPEAN CRISIS

The position of the Swedish foreign exchange market was, therefore, highly sensitive during the late spring of 1931. At this time events occurred abroad which later were to have a decisive influence upon the Swedish banking system. In May, 1931, the breakdown of the Credit Anstalt, in Vienna, caused a severe strain on foreign money centers. The German Reichsbank found itself compelled to raise its official bank rate from five to seven per cent in order to protect its own market. This action caused widespread distrust and foreigners began to withdraw their funds from German banks. This led the Reichsbank to increase its rediscount rate to 15 per cent; several German banks were closed and the government of the Reich had to impose severe foreign exchange restrictions. Germany was granted a moratorium on her war debt installments, and the "standstill" agreement was successfully negotiated. About 90 million kronor of Swedish funds were involved in this agreement.

The German confidence crisis brought a further strain on the Swedish banking system. Foreign banks that had funds tied up in the German banks. were compelled to utilize whatever claims they possessed in other countries, and so the Swedish banks suddenly began to lose large amounts of short-term foreign bank deposits. During June, July, and August of 1931, the Swedish banks paid out no less than 216 million kronor to foreign banks To this must also be added withdrawals on private accounts, a combination which resulted in a severe drain on the foreign exchange reserve of the Bank of Sweden and of the commercial banks. At the end of August, 1931, the Bank of Sweden had only 127 million kronor of foreign exchange reserve left. The commercial banks also had lost about 50 millions of their holdings of foreign exchange.

THE SITUATION DURING THE LATE SUMMER OF 1931

The general economic situation during the late summer was, therefore, as follows: (1) commodity imports exceeded exports; (2) short term capital movements had made an about turn; (3) the chaotic conditions abroad brought increased strain to the Swedish market; (4) Kreuger payments abroad continued. Such a situation could evidently be upheld only so long as Sweden possessed, or by borrowing could obtain, foreign exchange. In the meantime something had to be done to bring about equilibrium in the balance of international payments, either by curtailing the outflow of capital or by diminishing the excess of commodity imports. The Bank of Sweden therefore raised the official bank rate from three to four per cent on July 31, and on September 21 it further increased the rate to five per cent, and four days later to six per cent. This was not sufficient to stop the efflux of capital, as conditions abroad compelled owners of foreign funds to withdraw them, and high bank rates no longer attracted foreign investors. The only remaining alternative which could bring about equilibrium was therefore to deflate domestic prices and wages; but the social and industrial consequences of such action compelled the authorities to abstain. When on September 21, the Bank of England suspended gold payments, the effect on Sweden was pronounced. The fact that the krona previously had followed the pound sterling caused increased distrust abroad in the stability of the Swedish financial structure, and foreign funds left the Swedish banks at an accelerated pace. Foreign exchange was thus brought to a low ebb. The Bank of Sweden, which had also lost about 12 millions of kronor in gold, partly because of the domestic drain, had only 38 millions left. The only possible method remaining of achieving the necessary equilibrium was to borrow abroad.

A few days before Great Britain suspended gold payments, the Bank of England informed the Governors of the Bank of Sweden of the coming change of standard in England. The Bank of Sweden thus given time to consider means of protection, was saved an unpleasant surprise. On the fifth of September attempts had already been made to obtain foreign loans through the Public Debt Office for the Bank of Sweden. Loan negotiations were carried on in New York and later also in Paris. Upon *de facto* suspension in England, a meeting was called in Stockholm of representatives of the large commercial and private banks, the Bank of Sweden, and the government. At this meeting it was decided that all possible means should be employed to prevent a suspension of gold payments. The Stock Exchange was closed on September 21 to prevent an acceleration of the demands for foreign exchange through imports of securities. At the same time loan negotiations were speeded up. The drain on the foreign exchange reserve of the central bank, however, continued at an increased pace, particularly since it was rumored that the New York banks were unwilling to extend any credit for purposes of stabilizing the Swedish krona. On Saturday, September 26, a definite report of refusal came from New York, and on the following day from Paris also. From the twenty-first to the twenty-sixth the Bank of Sweden's holdings of gold and foreign exchange decreased by about a hundred million kronor. Thus, on Sunday, the twenty-seventh, the Bank's gold holdings had dwindled to a mere 198 millions, while the reserve of foreign exchange had shrunk to approximately 30 millions! A further decline of the gold stock would have made it impossible to fulfill the legal gold reserve requirements stipulated for the Bank of Sweden by Parliament. A meeting was called at Stockholm in which the Governors of the Banks of Norway, Denmark, Finland, and Sweden participated. At this meeting consideration was given to the feasibility of forming a monetary bloc for mutual protection along lines similar to those of the discarded Scandinavian monetary union, which had been established during the troubled times preceding the World War. The Governors of the Banks of Denmark and Finland expressed determination to adhere to gold at all costs, while Sweden, recognizing the impossibility of remaining on gold, decided to relieve the Bank of Sweden of its responsibility of gold payments. At the same time exports of gold were prohibited.

In conjunction with the suspension of gold payments on September 27, 1931, the government declared that its future monetary policy was to have, as its objective, the *preservation of the domestic purchasing power of the krona.*

It is necessary here to interrupt our narrative and to pause for a consideration of some of the economic problems that arise out of a change from gold to inconvertible paper currency. The following chapter will be devoted to a discussion of these problems, and an attempt will be made at the same time to throw some light upon the highly important question of *objectives* for a managed currency policy.

CHAPTER IV

A Few Elementary Concepts

Ordinarily, economic life goes on on the assumption of a fixed value of money. Men usually concern themselves about the values of goods, and take the value of money for granted. They seek to buy in the cheapest market and they seek to sell in the dearest market. Buying, they are glad to save all the money that they can. Selling, they are glad to get all the money that they can. What they aim at is, as far as possible, a surplus of money when the transactions are over, money that they trust and take for granted. When, however, the value of the money itself comes into question, and men are uncertain as to what money will be worth a week hence, a month hence, a year hence or longer, a new complication arises and a new set of reactions manifests itself.[1]

With a country still "on gold," business men can freely undertake obligations without any fear as to the future value of money, but as soon as gold payments are suspended, the problem of the future value of money begins to interfere with their calculations. Then, the average business man discovers that money and credit have a fluctuating value "of their own," and there often occurs a flight of

[1] Dr. Benjamin M. Anderson, Jr. in *The Chase Economic Bulletin.* Vol. XIII, No. 4, (December 13, 1933).

money into goods, simply because it is feared that money will decrease in value, and prices will go up. It may well happen, however, that the reverse process takes place. Instead of depreciating, the value of the currency may rise, causing a flight from goods into money; in other words, a rush to sell, with deflation rather than inflation as the disturbing element. Yet the first possibility is the most commonly feared; at times to such an extent that this fear brings about the very situation that everybody wants to avoid, as was the case when the United States suspended gold payments. At that time, judging from the favorable position of the United States' international balance of payments, the dollar was actually undervalued in the international market; but immediately after the suspension of the gold standard, foreign exchange quotations began to show that a flight of capital away from the domestic market was taking place. Instead of rising in value, the dollar fell, because of the *fear* of depreciation.

Such occurrences as the one just described are too commonplace to warrant further discussion. They have been mentioned simply because they show that *confidence* in the future value of money suddenly disappears when gold is no longer available in exchange for bills and notes. Confidence, particularly in the value of money, is an essential factor in economic life, and when it disappears through the suspension of gold payments, it becomes the *duty* of the government to reëstablish it by *announcing and adhering to a definite objective in its monetary policy*. A definite objective of this kind should, of course, always exist even when a country is "on gold," but when the money unit of a country is no longer "tied to gold," a definite policy is not merely valuable but, indeed, essential.

MANAGEMENT OF MONEY

When such a monetary policy is announced, it is commonly held that the government ventures upon a "managed currency" program. The term "managed currency" is, therefore (inaccurately, as we shall see), used to designate such monetary policies as are undertaken when a country is on an inconvertible paper standard. It seems to be a widespread belief that the functions which are performed by the technique of central banking in times of adherence to the gold standard are purely automatic. This common misconception is very likely due to the fact that central banking policies are not publicly announced when a country is on the gold standard. However, there is no principle distinction between management of money and credit when a country is "on" or "off" the gold standard. The objectives of such management might perhaps differ, although that is not necessary, while the technique of management remains the same in both cases.

On the subject of central banking policies there exist several schools of thought. One maintains that the objective of such policies should be to uphold the liquidity of the money market and to protect the domestic as well as foreign value of the currency; while other thinkers on the subject advocate such objectives as: e.g., stable wholesale prices, gradually falling prices, or slowly rising prices. Whatever difference there is between these schools of thought, however, they have one thing in common and that is a desire to obtain as high a degree of material happiness—"prosperity"—as possible.

When a country is still "on gold" the aims of central banking policies may not always be explicitly defined; consciously, the banking authorities may follow an objective designed merely to smooth out such money and credit obstacles as may lie in the path of the normal course of trade and production, while in doing so it may well occur that the objective in reality is one of influencing price movements. In some countries and under certain conditions, the central banks have also attempted to influence the cyclical fluctuations of business and industry, and have also exercised a guardianship over foreign trade, as well as over the flow of short-term and long-term capital funds. But as long as the gold standard is still adhered to, the objectives of central banking operations are commonly less well defined than they must be when a country is on an inconvertible paper standard.

THE MONETARY TOOLS ARE THE SAME IN BOTH CASES

It should be noted, also, that there is no distinction, in principle, between the monetary means which the central banking authorities have at their disposal when a country is "on gold" and when the gold standard is suspended. The tools, in both cases, are, therefore: the official bank rate, the open market operations (wherever the central institution is empowered to undertake such operations), operations in the foreign exchange market (provided the bank's charter gives such privileges), and moral suasion.[2]

The efficacy of these tools is not the same in every country. In Sweden, for example, where the commercial banks are normally indebted to the central institution, changes in the bank rate (primarily upward changes) exercise a great deal of influence upon credit extension by the banking community. It is also reasonable to maintain that the more centralized a banking system is, the greater is the power of central banking operations over the policies of the commercial banks. The management of money and credit is, therefore, more likely to fulfill the objectives in a country having a centralized banking system, than it is in a country in which the banking system is decentralized or diffused. But even if we consider merely a national economy with centralized banking, we must bear in mind the *limitations* of purely monetary influence over the

[2] The reader should be aware that all non-monetary means, such as tariffs, and export and import quota systems are omitted, as they properly belong to the sphere of government and not to central banking, and because, although the term "government" appears in this discussion, the treatment of all other than purely monetary means is excluded. It should, also, be recognized that the author makes no distinction between the "central bank" and the "government," although these institutions are not always coöperating to the fullest extent. However, it is difficult to see how it can be possible for the central bank authorities in any country to refuse to follow, in times of stress, a monetary program promulgated by the government. It, therefore, matters little whether the term central bank or government is used in outlining the means which a *nation* has at its disposal to carry out its financial objectives.

developments of the economic structure as a whole. No matter how well defined a monetary program might be, it cannot, as we shall see from the experience of Sweden, control all other economic factors under all circumstances. In general, it seems to be quite obvious from the experiences of many countries during this depression, that it is far easier to hamper economic developments, than it is to *cause* greater economic activity by the application of purely monetary means, the management of money and credit. Banks cannot lend funds to their customers unless the customers are willing to borrow! And it is, also, quite obvious that a country cannot raise its general price level simply by raising the price of gold in terms of the domestic currency.[3]

SUGGESTIONS FOR OBJECTIVES

The need for a definite objective for the monetary policies of a country no longer adhering to the gold standard has already been pointed out; and we shall now examine some suggestions for such an objective. For the sake of simplicity we may divide them into two groups. The first one we may term "international," and the second one "domestic." Obviously, there is no way in which the "international" and the "domestic" objectives can be completely separated from one another. They are always more or less interrelated. The degree of interconnection depends upon the economic structure of the country concerned, as well as on the nature of its foreign relations.

[3] For a further discussion of this, see *The Chase Economic Bulletin*, Vol. XIII, No. 4.

The economic mechanism which usually becomes most visibly disturbed by the renunciation of gold payments is the foreign exchange market. Fluctuations in the foreign value of the domestic currency are then no longer limited by the "upper" and "lower" gold points, as gold is not available as a means of settling international payments. The volume and price of the visible and invisible items entering into the international exchange of the country, together with speculative factors, determine the rate at which the domestic currency is quoted in terms of the moneys of other nations. Obviously, heavy fluctuations in the foreign exchange rates may then occur, deterring the flow of goods and services in and out of the country; and it is, therefore, quite in order that the government, seeking to maintain or restore a fair degree of normal economic intercourse with foreign countries, should undertake to preserve, as far as possible, the stability of its currency in the international markets

The government may, also, follow a policy of depreciation of the international value of its currency. Such a program is often defended by saying that it will favor the export trade of the country. Be that as it may, the depreciation of the external value of the currency can hardly be continued over a long span of time, even if other governments do not retaliate with similar measures, as by favoring exports the government, also and automatically, hampers imports. Ultimately, the consumers of the country, the currency of which is being depreciated in the foreign exchange markets, have to pay for the favors thus granted to the export industries. The degree to which the individual consumer pays depends upon the extent to which he purchases imported goods. This is, of course, under the assumption that rising prices for imported articles have not had time to operate first on related prices and later on the price structure as a whole. If, however, this occurs, all consumers share more or less equally in the burden.

Disregarding the burden placed on the consumers, we may contend that a small country with a large volume of foreign trade relative to its domestic trade has a better opportunity of making a policy of depreciation of the external value of the currency effective, than has a nation to which the foreign trade is of comparatively little importance. This holds true, also, with regard to foreign retaliation, as a policy of depreciation is more apt to meet counteracting currency policies from abroad if it is undertaken by a large rather than a small country. Foreign hostility, however, cannot be overlooked by either a small or a large nation.

CONTROL OVER HOME MARKET

The government may, also, center its attention on the purely domestic market, leaving the foreign exchange rates to fluctuate according to the pressure exercised by domestic and foreign factors—be they "trade" or "speculative." The government then follows a monetary policy, which, in the absence of a better term, may be said to seek the fulfillment of a "domestic objective." Such an aim may be the achievement of stability of wholesale prices, a slow rise of such prices in the interest of domestic productivity, a lowering of general prices as a means to facilitate exports, the preservation of purchasing power on the domestic market, or even maintenance of liquidity in the money market with the end in view of facilitating domestic business activity. All of these objectives may be classified as a desire on the part of the government to preserve, restore, or improve the country's internal economy.

A so-called "price level" is merely an average of a great number of prices, and although, as we shall note in the following chapter, it is expedient to formulate an objective for a managed currency policy in terms of prices, it should be borne in mind that stable wholesale prices (an index of such prices) do not by themselves stimulate economic development and prosperity. Prosperity is largely the effect of an interplay of economic factors facilitated by the existence of an equilibrium of the *entire* price structure, and not merely by the stability of a certain group of representative prices. Neither do stable wholesale prices mean stability in the general purchasing power of the money unit. Indeed, an ideally perfect unit of general purchasing power is not merely unattainable; it is, according to the late Professor Alfred Marshall, unthinkable, for the effective value of money to each individual depends partly on the nature of his wants.

Furthermore, wholesale prices are composed of three groups of prices: domestic, import, and export wholesale prices. To achieve stability of the average of *all* wholesale prices is, therefore, most difficult, as export and import prices are directly influenced by conditions in both the domestic and the foreign markets. The government can hardly exercise any appreciable influence over price movements abroad, but has to limit itself to the domestic market and the foreign exchange rates, the latter, however, not being the only determining factors of prices of export and import goods. Thus, even if the average of domestic wholesale prices remains tolerably stable, the aggregate of wholesale prices may fluctuate widely because of the influence of the prices of export and import goods. Obviously, coincidence might come to the rescue by offsetting the effect of export and import prices, whereby an average of all wholesale prices may remain constant.

Without elaborating on all the problems inherent in every one of the objectives suggested here, it should be emphasized that some *definite* objective is essential in order to avert complete economic chaos under a system of "managed currency." Although an objective may not reach its fulfillment it serves, nevertheless, as a guide for the monetary policy itself, and also as a means of gaining the confidence of the general public in the future value of the currency, to whatever degree that is possible when the gold standard is suspended.

CHAPTER V

The Initial Objective and Its Principal Guide

It was pointed out at the end of Chapter III that the Swedish government announced, on the very day the gold standard was abandoned, that the monetary policy would thereafter be directed toward the preservation of the internal purchasing power of the krona. This meant that the Government had decided to center its attention on the domestic market, without, however, neglecting to consider the external value of the Swedish currency.

Vague as such a program may seem at first glance, the announcement was, nevertheless, of the utmost significance. This may be more fully understood if we take into account some of the possible aims which the government, by implication, excluded.

A RETURN TO GOLD IMPRACTICABLE

When contemplating the course which the government chose to follow, we should bear in mind that the abandonment of gold had been caused, mainly, by forces over which the Swedish government could hardly have been able to exercise any control from within the country. This is most important to recognize, as it refutes the belief, for some time current abroad, that Sweden, largely because of strains on the domestic market, had been compelled to suspend the gold standard.

For a country such as Sweden, relying heavily upon foreign trade, the external value of the currency exercises a great influence on the domestic price structure. The abandonment of gold does, therefore, present a variety of problems, the solution of which should in large measure determine the future development of the domestic price structure.

In principle it would have been quite logical for the Swedish government to decide upon a monetary policy leading to a speedy return to some international money standard. The only existing international standard was gold, and yet, so long as large volumes of short-term capital moved from country to country upon the least provocation, gold could hardly be regarded as a universal standard likely to remain intact. It would, moreover, have been impracticable to return to gold at the old parity, as such a move would necessarily have involved a further deflation of domestic prices, which would in turn have been likely to cause serious disturbances in the labor market, thereby adversely affecting the productivity of domestic industries. A return to gold at the old parity would also have been tantamount to class favoritism, the consequences of which would have still further complicated the situation.

The only possible method of returning to gold would, therefore, have been to "tie" the krona to the gold currencies at some other mint par of exchange. Advocates of such a policy were not lacking. Yet the future status of gold was regarded as most uncertain; furthermore, such a policy would have implied that the Swedish banking system, and particularly the central bank, had a substantial amount of foreign balances at its disposal to safeguard the new mint parity. Such, however, was not the case; hence it was regarded as of little avail, if not altogether impossible, to attempt a return to gold even at some new parity.

DANGER OF "PEGGING" THE KRONA TO THE POUND STERLING

One of the reasons that caused Sweden to leave the gold standard was the policy followed by the central bank of directing the external value of the krona so as to conform closely to the movements of the international value of the pound sterling. It was decided, now however, to maintain the krona independent of the pound, as it was feared that by "pegging" the Swedish currency to the pound the Swedish price structure might be adversely influenced in the event of price distortions in Great Britain.

Inasmuch as all attempts to obtain foreign loans for foreign exchange transactions had failed, because of the general uncertainty prevailing in all money centers, Sweden was left to care for the international value of her currency without even a reasonable volume of foreign exchange at the disposal of the Bank of Sweden, while the excess of commodity imports over exports showed no tendency to abate.

Since, for reasons of expediency arising out of the internal economic situation, the Swedish currency had to be kept independent both of gold and of the

British currency, the problem resolved itself into deciding at just what level the external value of the krona should be maintained. Such a level had to be sought with two things in mind, the internal price structure and the trends of the external values of foreign currencies. To clarify this problem it is necessary to talk in terms of price levels.

To maintain constant a certain level of prices or even to keep the trend of an index of prices unchanged does not of itself imply that the price structure as a whole is kept in balance, as maladjustments may well occur within the price structure. As we shall see later, however, an index of prices may well serve as a guide and as a criterion of monetary policy. A criterion of this kind is the more expedient because the general public is habitually interested in the movement of prices. This being the case, the formulation of a monetary policy in terms of prices no doubt helps the central bank authorities to gain the understanding and confidence of the business community, without which it is extremely difficult to make monetary tools effective.

But even if the program is expressed in terms of some group of prices, it is quite possible for the monetary authorities, while using an index of prices as a guide, to have a broader and perhaps less concrete aim. Such aims might be: e.g., insuring the profitableness of industry and trade, or maintaining the standard of living of certain classes of people or of the community as a whole. In order to attain such a goal, however, the monetary policy must be based upon the prevailing economic and social conditions of the country; furthermore, it must be directed as far as feasible (through transactions in the foreign exchange market) so as to avert disturbances in the home market from price distortions abroad. The degree to which prices in the international markets are likely to influence economic developments at home is largely dependent upon the volume of exports and imports. To a country like Sweden the trend of prices abroad is of great importance, because of the comparative significance of her foreign trade. This problem, however, is somewhat simplified by the custom of remitting payments for Swedish foreign trade, mainly imports, in one currency, the pound sterling. Even the most skilful handling of the external value of the krona, however, cannot by any means save the country from the influence of adverse price trends in foreign markets, particularly during a period when most currencies are detached from gold.

NECESSITY OF MAINTAINING PRODUCTION

Upon the announcement by the government of its intention to preserve the purchasing power of the Swedish currency the necessity of maintaining and if possible increasing domestic production was, at least by implication, immediately apparent. This was more or less self-evident, as the aim of the government, expressed in other words, simply meant that the standard of living was to be kept unimpaired. It was therefore necessary not merely to maintain production, but also to insure, so far as that is feasible through monetary means, the profitableness of production, in order to maintain wages and to prevent disturbances in the labor market. Because of the excess of imports over exports, strikes or other labor conflicts, particularly in the export industries, would have left a still greater "gap" in the balance of international payments than the one already existing. Labor conflicts, therefore, if for no other than purely monetary reasons, had to be avoided. That it was not possible to avert such disturbances entirely will be shown in Chapter VII.

Under the then prevailing conditions there were only two ways in which production could be maintained: first by increasing the price of the goods produced, and secondly, by lowering costs of production. The first alternative is passed over here as it is taken up later in this discussion; as to the second alternative, a lowering of wages was hardly feasible, for reasons given above. As far as other elements of costs were concerned, only those that were solely dependent upon domestic economic factors could be lowered. Such imported materials as enter into the production of domestic goods, for example, could hardly be made to command a lower price in terms of the krona unless the external value of the currency in relation to the currency of the exporting country was raised substantially, a measure which could not be introduced if Swedish exporters were to have a fair opportunity to compete with foreign exporters in the international market.

There remained, however, the possibility of raising domestic wholesale prices without, at the same time, bringing about an increase in the cost of living. This was due to the fact that retail prices had not declined to the same extent as wholesale prices. The existence of this disparity made it possible at least to formulate a monetary policy aimed at a gradual rise in domestic wholesale prices as a means of stimulating domestic production.

Although the initial program merely stressed the desire to preserve the internal purchasing power of the general public, the need for the maintenance of production, and tranquillity in the labor market were essential, although merely implied, features of the program.

THE CONSUMPTION PRICE INDEX OF THE BANK OF SWEDEN

In order to measure the purchasing power of the krona in the hands of a representative cross-section of the entire community, a consumption price index was constructed. Materials for price statistics were collected under the supervision of the Bank of Sweden, so that

> at any moment information would be available of actual price tendencies and it would be possible to judge the effects of the Bank's monetary policy and the measures which might be necessitated for the fulfillment of its monetary programme.[1]

The statistical department of the Bank of Sweden computes this index. Assistance in collecting the material is rendered by the Board of Trade and the

[1] This and subsequent quotations appearing in the discussion of this index are drawn from a mimeographed memorandum prepared (April, 1933) by Erik Lindahl, professor in the University of Commerce, Gothenburg. Italics mine.

Royal Social Board as well as by some private agencies.

These price statistics are formulated partly in a *weekly* table of the whole commodity price system and partly in a *weekly* index of the average retail prices of the goods and services which enter into the consumption of the community.

From the prices obtained through the above mentioned sources an index number is calculated in such a way that it will enable the Bank of Sweden to detect

as far as possible both the *origin* of price changes and their importance for agriculture and industry.

In each category of commodities there are thus included both representative foreign price quotations (both in gold and sterling currencies) and the corresponding Swedish export and import prices, and also prices in the wholesale and retail trade in Stockholm in connection with these goods or their products. By comparing these various quotations it is possible to decide how far an internal price movement is dependent upon foreign price changes or an alteration in the exchanges, and how far it is founded on more internal conditions, for example, a change in home demand. Since the commodity items are grouped as necessities and products of agriculture and industry respectively, it is possible to form a conception as to how far price movements have influenced the profitableness of these branches of production.

This index, however, is by no means the only index which the Bank of Sweden employs to guide its monetary policy. It also makes use of wholesale price indices published by the commercial banks and the Royal Board of Trade, as well as of the price series relating to raw materials and products, which are of importance from the point of view of the profitableness of production.

The aim of the consumption price index is to register at short intervals in the most generally comprehensible and widely applicable way possible the influence of Swedish monetary policy with regard to the internal purchasing power of the krona, for the information both of the directors of the Bank of Sweden and the Swedish public. The index series is thus connected with the programme for monetary policy given above and is also intended to be of use in fixing this programme more in detail.

Data were assembled from fifteen localities to show the retail price of essential goods and services, which were considered representative of consumption within the entire country. The already existing indices of prices were mainly wholesale price indices. Furthermore they were published at long intervals of time, usually once a month. Nor were other existing retail price indices suitable from the point of monetary policy, as they are published monthly, while the index of cost of living, computed by the Royal Social Board, is a quarterly index. These indices therefore, throw only unsatisfactory light upon the prevailing price situation at any given moment and the information they convey is not sufficient as an estimate of the average domestic purchasing power of the Swedish currency.

Wholesale prices are dominated to a high degree by international staple commodities and thus to a great extent reflect only foreign price movements and the fluctuations of the exchanges. In estimating the average domestic price level however, more attention must be paid to the cost of commodities and services, the prices of which are largely determined by purely internal influences. In this respect the cost of living index is better, since in principle it also includes the prices of home prepared products and services. Neither is this index, however, an ideal one, partly because it is limited to the consumption of people at a certain level of income (2,000 kronor a year in 1914) and partly because it is based on a budget which is adapted for comparison with an earlier price level and accordingly does not fully correspond to the actual situation. Thus for the reasons given, hardly any of the index series mentioned constitute a suitable foundation for a more detailed fixing of the norm for Swedish monetary policy.

The Bank of Sweden index would, however, be less than reasonably representative, were it not for the fact that it is subjected to a constant process of resampling so as to adjust it to fundamental changes taking place in the commodity and service markets. The component parts of the index are thus altered as the need for change arises. The seasonal element in the availability of certain goods and services, as well as random alterations in the habits of the consumers, are consequently reflected in the index. The weighting of each component part is also changed from time to time so as to reflect, as far as feasible, the direction of effective consumer's demand. This index is, therefore, conspicuously different from the ordinary measures of cost of living, which are commonly intended to portray changes in the cost of living within a certain class of the community, notably the industrial working class. As far as it is possible, the present index of the Bank of Sweden "facilitates the study of the special price movements which collectively constitute the total price movement."

This index is thus intended to facilitate the determination of the monetary policy of the Bank of

Sweden, but obviously gives no information as to the policy itself.

It will only be possible to determine this when rules have been established for the regulation of the index series in question by measures of monetary policy. Under the present conditions this important question has so far only received a provisional and somewhat elastic solution. In accordance with the declarations of policy the directors of the Bank of Sweden therefore might have deemed it suitable to follow a policy which means *inter alia* that the consumption price level, as it is expressed in the index series under discussion, should not be kept absolutely unchanged.

Among the "allowable divergences" we may mention price changes due to "alterations in *indirect taxation*," seasonal price changes, and also

other changes of the consumption price level which are not conditional upon the construction of the index number but are of a more fundamental character. The allowable deviation from the unaltered price level has for the present, however, only been provisionally fixed in relation to the present situation; the consumption price level may deviate "within narrow limits" from the average level during 1931 insofar as measures to mitigate the depression necessitate such deviations.

CHAPTER VI

Progress of Events During the Latter Part of 1931

The suspension of the gold standard was an event which some weeks earlier very few people would have anticipated. While the general public was taken by surprise, the change of standard nevertheless met with general approval throughout the country. During the war and after it, thanks to the brilliant writings of leading Swedish political economists and a number of well-informed articles in the Swedish press, the general public had been educated to take a keen interest in problems of monetary policy. Now that these problems had once more been thrust into the foreground, public opinion had, therefore, been prepared to deal with them.[1]

Although the general public voiced approval of the policy of the government, it recognized that the program was merely of an emergency character, as Sweden had been forced off gold and as the Minister of Finance declared that it was the desire of the government to return to gold as soon as conditions abroad permitted.

In order to preserve the internal purchasing power of the krona, it at once became necessary to remove all fears of inflation. Had the government left open the road to currency or credit inflation, it would have been impossible to carry out its objec-

[1] The Skandinaviska Kreditaktiebolaget, *Quarterly Report*, October, 1931.

tive, as preservation of purchasing power and monetary inflation are clearly incompatible. In other words, the authorities recognized that the uncertainty that springs from anticipation of depreciation of the money unit would have to be eliminated in order to make possible the preservation of the internal buying power of the krona. Consequently the rediscount rate was raised from six to eight per cent, a step which, it was calculated, would have a twofold effect. It was hoped, first, that a severe decline in the international value of the krona would be prevented, and secondly, that any attempt towards speculative buying of goods and securities would be curtailed. It was felt that this exceptionally high rate would serve as a signal, both at home and abroad, that the government was determined to maintain as far as feasible the existing level of prices.

This measure might not have been entirely free of danger had there been a substantial volume of short-term foreign balances in the Stockholm market. A rise in the official bank rate of a country at that particular time, generally regarded by foreign interests as a sign of weakness, often caused withdrawals of short-term balances. However, as the major part of short-term foreign balances had already been withdrawn from the Stockholm market, and only a minimum of working balances remained, little could be feared from a rise of the bank rate. On the other hand, the foreign exchange reserve of the Bank of Sweden was at such a low ebb that little influence upon the movements of foreign exchanges could be expected from this source. Thus, an increase in the bank rate became the most logical measure to prevent a heavy decline of the krona in the foreign exchange market.

The first measure was, therefore, aimed at averting inflation. The next step came in the form of an agreement between the Bank of Sweden and the commercial banks, wherein the latter promised to exercise especial caution in their credit accommodations, particularly in the credit extended for import purposes.

In spite of the rise in the bank rate, a substantial lowering of the foreign value of the krona took place after the suspension of gold payments. The Bank of Sweden, however, made some attempt to steady the external value of the krona by sales of foreign exchange, causing a still further decline in the reserve of foreign exchange. That the authorities had no fear in selling foreign exchange, even when the balances were at a minimum, shows that they were determined to protect the value of the currency by all the means at their disposal. When, after the first shock, the gyrations in the foreign exchange market had steadied down somewhat, and it was known that in the immediate future no substantial withdrawals from the commercial banks on foreign accounts were to be expected, the Bank of Sweden, which customarily sets the daily price of the krona in the foreign exchange market,[2] decided to quote the pound sterling at its old parity. This was done in the anticipation that, with a lessened demand for

[2] Cf. p. 15.

pounds, some private holders of sterling exchange would be willing to sell their holdings at the "old" rate. With the exception of a few days in November, the pound remained approximately at its old mint par of exchange throughout the remainder of the year. The gold currencies, however, appreciated substantially, the dollar reaching 5.59 kronor (mint par of exchange 3.73 kronor) on December 8.

The reserves of foreign exchange held in the Bank of Sweden fell to a low point of 19 millions on November 21, 1931. During the remainder of the year, however, the supply increased, reaching 49 millions at the end of 1931. It is worthy of note that the gold stock did not decline, but, on the contrary, increased, after the suspension of the gold standard; a loss of gold, however, took place in the period from October 24 to November 21, 1931. The monetary gold stock was then 206 millions, the lowest point reached.[3] From then on, the gold reserve of the Bank of Sweden remained constant until March, 1933, when the Bank of Sweden began to increase its gold supply through purchases both at home and abroad. It should also be noted that the volume of money in circulation declined only very slightly during the latter part of 1931.

AMAZING STABILITY IN PRICES

The decline in the foreign value of the krona did not seem to influence however the domestic price level to any appreciable extent. It has been pointed out by Professor Ohlin that

[3] This refers to the period September, 1931-January, 1934.

it is a remarkable fact that so substantial a rise as over 40 per cent in the exchange rates of gold currencies had only a very slight effect on commodity prices in Sweden. Svenska Handelsbanken's index of import prices (1913 = 100) rose from 80 in September to 91 in December. The small proportion of the increase is to be explained partly by continually falling prices in the gold countries, partly by the fact that a number of Sweden's leading import goods, whether bought in England or elsewhere, are paid for in sterling. As regards Swedish export prices, the fact that both England, Denmark, Norway, and Finland had seen their currencies depreciate to about the same extent as the Swedish krona probably goes a long way toward explaining why the expected rise did not take place. The index number only rose from 111 to 113. As, moreover, the price level of domestic goods remained practically constant, the rise of the total wholesale price level was inconsiderable. Retail prices remained practically unaltered, and the cost of living even fell a little.[4]

That the internal purchasing power of the currency had been maintained practically constant may be seen from Table IV (page 58) showing the changes per *week* in the Bank of Sweden index from October 11 to the turn of the year.

In regard to exports during the latter part of 1931, there was some improvement, particularly in the trade with countries still adhering to gold. Exports of timber and other forest products to France and Holland had, however, already begun to improve before the suspension of the gold standard. The general trend of prices for bonds was downward during the last months of 1931, mainly because of the exceptionally high bank rate. Stock prices, on the other hand, remained fairly stable.

[4] Svenska Handelsbanken, *Index*, Vol. VII, No. 81 (September, 1931).

TABLE IV

WEEKLY CHANGES IN THE BANK OF SWEDEN INDEX, OCTOBER 11 TO DECEMBER 27, 1931

	INDEX NUMBER PER EACH PRECEDING WEEK = 100	SEPTEMBER 1931 = 100
October 11	99.39	99.39
October 18	99.96	99.34
October 25	100.06	99.40
November 1	99.97	99.37
November 8	100.23	99.60
November 15	100.09	99.70
November 22	100.25	99.95
November 29	100.04	99.99
December 6	100.07	100.06
December 13	99.97	100.03
December 20	99.98	100.01
December 27	100.04	100.06

As a whole the results obtained during this first period of the monetary program are, indeed, amazing, particularly in view of the simplicity of the monetary policy. The Bank of Sweden had done whatever it could to stabilize the external value of the krona in terms of pound sterling and it had on October 8 already lowered the bank rate from eight to seven per cent. On the nineteenth of the same month, the rate was further lowered to six per cent. In addition, the commercial banks had exercised a cautious credit policy, partly because of a desire on their part to improve their liquidity, but also in order to conform to the above-mentioned agreement. Furthermore, some foreign exchange restrictions aimed at preventing, as far as possible, speculation in foreign exchange and in goods were imposed. But such foreign exchange restrictions as did exist in Sweden during the autumn of 1931 are not to be compared with the severe restrictions that were imposed in other European countries at the time.

No doubt, as pointed out by Professor Ohlin, there were many factors of coincidence; therefore one cannot say that it was merely the monetary policies of the Bank of Sweden that preserved the purchasing power of the krona in the hands of the consumers, particularly in view of the fact that the index of the Bank of Sweden was not available as a guide until several weeks after the suspension of the gold standard. It cannot be denied, however, that both the central bank authorities and the leaders of the commercial banks did everything in their power to avert a further distortion of prices. Whether it would have been possible for them to succeed had they been compelled to labor under unfortunate rather than fortunate circumstances, is, of course, a query of purely theoretical interest.

CHAPTER VII

Monetary Program Revised

Thus the situation looked quite hopeful when Parliament convened in January, 1932. The Minister of Finance then proposed a revision of the monetary policy. He emphasized the fact that stabilization of the purchasing power of the krona should apply to the broad consumer class and that, as it had been proven possible to "confine within narrow limits fluctuations in the internal value of the Swedish krona, especially its purchasing power in the hands of the consumers," an attempt should now be made to achieve a slow rise of wholesale prices in order to "stimulate the economic activities of the country without giving rise to any danger of inflation." It was also proposed that the Bank of Sweden should attempt to limit, as far as possible, the fluctuations of the foreign exchanges. This had already been attempted, as we have seen, during the last quarter of 1931, although the Bank of Sweden was not at that time in a position to influence substantially the movements of the foreign exchanges. However, the central institution was now in a better position to cope with this problem; and it was, therefore, suggested that it do whatever it could to achieve a minimum of fluctuations.

Before considering in more detail this revised monetary policy, it is worth while to note a statement made by the Governors of the Bank of Sweden in February, 1932, wherein it was emphasized that, the Bank was *not* aiming at

maintaining unchanged the average retail price level for all consumers' goods. Through the rise in the prices of certain import and export goods, which may be expected gradually to be more and more strongly reflected in the retail market, such a monetary policy would necessitate a corresponding forcing down of the prices of home-market goods—a development that would intensify the crisis in Sweden. The aforesaid pronouncement should rather be taken to imply that the *Riksbank's* intention is to endeavour to maintain more or less unaltered the average level of prices of home-market goods and of the most important services that form an integral part of consumption. A monetary policy along these lines is compatible with a certain rise in the *Riksbank's* index, viz. insofar as it might be caused by a rise in import and export prices (and prices directly dependent thereon) brought about by a rise in exchange rates and in commodity prices abroad . . . . It follows that when forming its policy in view of fluctuations in the price level the *Riksbank* cannot but take into account the causes of such changes in prices. For it is essential to determine whether price movements are caused, e.g., by increased tariffs, altered exchange rates or a tendency to inflation on the domestic market which may be looked upon as primary in relation to exchange rates. In any such analysis of price conditions, naturally other price indices besides the *Riksbank's* own index of consumers' prices will also be taken into consideration. *Obviously, in their endeavour to create as stable economic conditions as possible, the Governors are also taking into account other factors than mere changes in the price level, particularly conditions affecting productivity and stocks in various industries.*[1]

The Government and the Diet postponed their decision until the beginning of May, when the Banking Committee submitted

[1] B. Ohlin, "Sweden's Monetary Policy," in Svenska Handelsbanken, *Index*, Vol. VII, No. 81, 1932. Italics mine.

its report to the Diet on the administration of the Riksbank. In this report the Committee states, inter alia, that "the efforts to regulate the value of the krona should take *as their starting-point the internal price level and the requirements of our own economic life.*" The Committee expresses the wish not only that a continued deflation be as actively combated as the feared inflation would have been, but also that there should be some recovery in wholesale prices, though there should be "no question of prices reverting to a level too far removed from the present one." Not merely import and export prices but also "the prices of home-market goods should obviously be permitted to rise, provided the cost of living is not seriously affected thereby." It was held that for the time being there should be no question of pegging the external value of the krona either to gold or to sterling.[2]

With the acceptance of this revised and well-defined policy, the government diverted substantially from its first aim, that of avoiding inflation, and now ventured to obtain a gradual rise in wholesale prices as a stimulant to domestic production and general economic activity within the country. At the same time exchange fluctuations were to be curtailed without, however, "pegging" the external value of the krona to any foreign currency.

In reality, the objective of the program was to adjust the wholesale price level to the prevailing costs of production. Wages and other costs had remained at a high level during the entire period of deflation. It should also be noted that the Banking Committee insisted that the anticipated rise should not be permitted to affect seriously the costs of living, as that would be tantamount to a depreciation of the internal purchasing power of the cur-

[2] *Ibid.* Italics mine.

rency. The price-raising program should, on the contrary, be kept within limits, so that prices should not revert "to a level too far removed from the present one." Furthermore, it is important to recognize that the Bank of Sweden, in attempting to minimize fluctuations in the foreign exchange market, and also in its efforts to influence the trend of the international value of the krona, decided to "take as its starting point the internal price level and the requirements of our own economic life." Thus, there was no desire to tie the krona to the currency of any foreign country, whether it was on or off the gold standard. To tie the krona to the gold currencies was held to imply deflation, and such a monetary policy should, the Banking Committee asserted, be combatted quite as vigorously as any inflationary tendencies. It is also interesting to observe that the Committee advised that the monetary policies should not be directed to conform, solely, to a certain index number. It was felt that no formal or simple rule could be given as a guide, but that the Bank of Sweden must take into account all those factors that influence the economic well-being of the entire country. It was also deemed desirable to keep interest rates at as low a level as possible, without, however, thereby hampering the objective of the program.

Although this program did not become effective until May, 1932, it is interesting to note that the rediscount rate which had been held at six per cent until February 19, was then lowered to five and a half per cent. On March 3 the rate was again lowered, this time to five per cent; but, as the Kreuger crisis prevented a further decline of the rate, it was not until May 17 that the rate reached four and a half per cent. Then, on June 3, a further change in the rate was made to four per cent, and on August 31 the rediscount rate was quoted at three and a half per cent, a rate which prevailed throughout the remainder of the year. Thus, except for the interruption due to the unforeseen occurrences in March, the Bank of Sweden followed a policy of continuously lowering its official bank rate. However, as the commercial banks adjusted merely their discount rate for commercial bills to the changes in the bank rate, while other interest rates were permitted to lag—the stimulating effect of constantly lowered interest rates was somewhat hampered, particularly as the savings banks kept their rates at a relatively high level.[3]

Before we turn to a study of the developments in the price structure during 1932, we must take into consideration the foreign exchange market. The Bank of Sweden's reserve of foreign exchange, which at the beginning of the year equaled 49 millions of kronor, increased substantially during the ensuing months, thereby enabling the Bank to influence the external value of the krona. That such an increase in the foreign exchange reserve of the Bank was possible, while commodity imports continued to exceed exports, is partly explained by the fact that in securities there was an excess of exports over imports, and also that payments of

[3] See Chart 1.

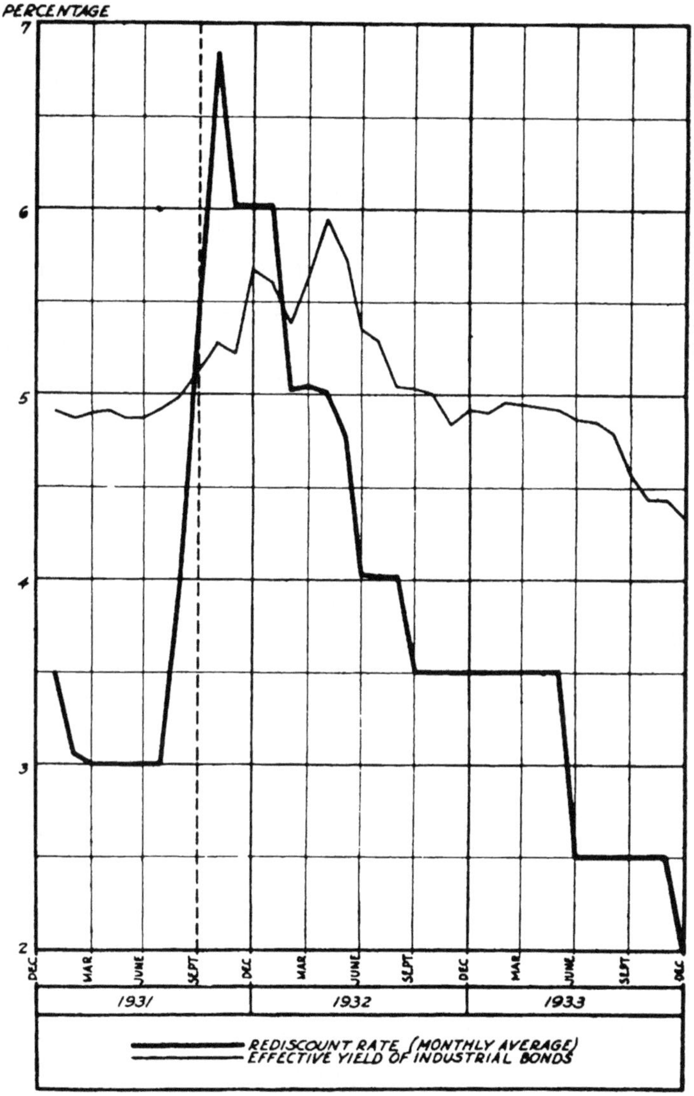

CHART I. CHANGES IN THE REDISCOUNT RATE (MONTHLY AVERAGES) AND EFFECTIVE YIELD OF INDUSTRIAL BONDS

Calculated on market prices at middle of months.

Source: The Skandinaviska Kreditaktiebolaget.

interest and dividends on foreign securities held in Sweden were being made.[4] Tables V and VI show first, the imports and exports of securities, by quarters; and second, the changes in supply of foreign exchange in the Bank of Sweden and the commercial banks, and the sum total of foreign exchange reserve at the disposal of the banking community. In the second table, monthly figures are presented. Both tables are taken from the report of the Banking Committee of Parliament, January 17, 1933, and show the changes in millions of kronor.

TABLE V

EXPORTS AND IMPORTS OF SECURITIES IN 1932

1932	IMPORTS OF SECURITIES	EXPORTS OF SECURITIES	EXCESS OF EXPORTS
First quarter	20	59	39
Second quarter	21	31	10
Third quarter	21	45	24
Fourth quarter	21	63	42
Total	83	198	115

With this increase in the supply of foreign exchange, it became possible for the Bank of Sweden to minimize exchange fluctuations. Table VII shows the monthly averages of the exchange rates in London and New York and also the dollar-pound relations. Since these figures are merely monthly averages, they do not give an adequate picture of the movements of the external value of the krona; they do, however, indicate that the Bank trans-

[4] For a more detailed discussion of this point see B. Ohlin, "The Inadequacy of Price Stabilization," in Svenska Handelsbanken, *Index*, Vol. VIII, No. 96.

TABLE VI

NET SUPPLY OF FOREIGN EXCHANGE

AT END OF	BANK OF SWEDEN	COM. BANKS	TOTAL
1931 December	49	240	289
1932 January	81	229	310
February	91	219	310
March	112	208	320
April	114	208	322
May	122	177	299
June	133	168	301
July	162	172	334
August	171	178	349
September	178	176	354
October	193	173	366
November	220	162	382
December	213	215	428

ferred the "level" of the pound-krona relation from one approximating the old par to a level of about 19.50 kronor to the pound sterling.[6] As to the reason for this policy, Professor Ohlin maintains that it was based on a

consideration of the monetary program that had been decided upon in May, in which the Riksbank was enjoined to prevent a further lowering of prices in Sweden and to bring about a certain rise in wholesale prices. As during the spring the wholesale price level had been sharply declining both in the gold countries and in England, and a certain tendency to falling prices had also been noticeable in Sweden, a fall in foreign exchange rates would obviously have caused the downward movement of prices in foreign markets to spread to Sweden with double force. It was inevitable, therefore, first to check the fall in exchange rates and then, as prices in other countries continued to decline, to effect a rise in order to neutralize the effect of falling prices abroad on Swedish import and export prices. The latter task was facilitated during the summer by

[6] See Chart 2.

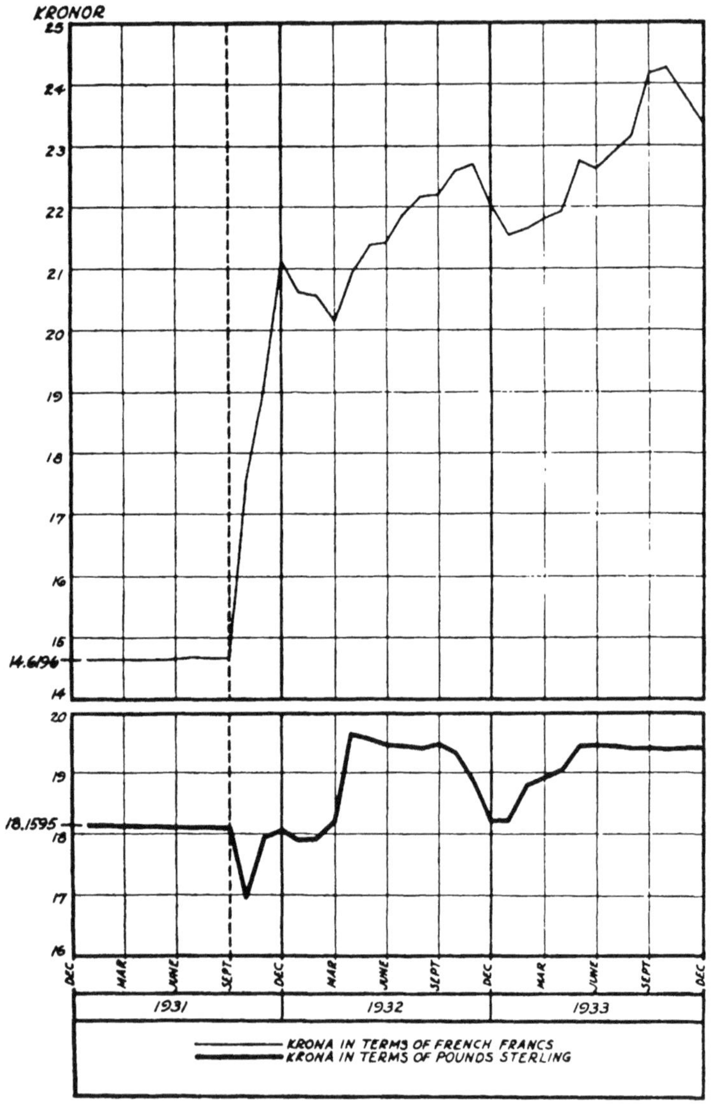

CHART 2. THE TREND OF THE KRONA IN TERMS OF THE POUND STERLING AND THE FRENCH FRANC.

At par 18,1595 kronor equal one pound sterling, and 14,6196 kronor equal 100 francs.

Source: The Skandinaviska Kreditaktiebolaget.

the depreciation of sterling in relation to gold. During July the gold exchange rates gradually rose, while the sterling rate was kept at a steady level of about Kr. 19.50. The result was that during August the gold value of the Swedish krona had fallen to 66½ per cent of par.[6]

The figures showing the net supply of foreign exchange point toward a substantial increase for the Bank of Sweden, indicating that a deliberate policy was in operation. The data for the commercial banks, however, show that they lost foreign exchange through the repayment of foreign credits.

TABLE VII

INTERRELATIONS OF THE POUND STERLING, KRONA, AND DOLLAR IN 1932

1932	POUND STERLING IN TERMS OF KRONOR	DOLLARS IN TERMS OF KRONOR	POUND STERLING IN TERMS OF DOLLARS
January	17.91	5.22	3.430
February	17.96	5.19	3.457
March	18.32	5.08	3.621
April	19.72	5.25	3.752
May	19.69	5.36	3.676
June	19.52	5.35	3.650
July	19.51	5.49	3.552
August	19.48	5.61	3.476
September	19.50	5.62	3.472
October	19.40	5.70	3.399
November	18.81	5.74	3.277
December	18.32	5.58	3.276

Let us now see what happened to the Swedish price structure during this year.[7]

From a study of Chart 4 it is quite evident that the objective of raising wholesale prices did not

[6] Svenska Handelsbanken, *Index*, Vol. VII, No. 81.
[7] See Chart 4.

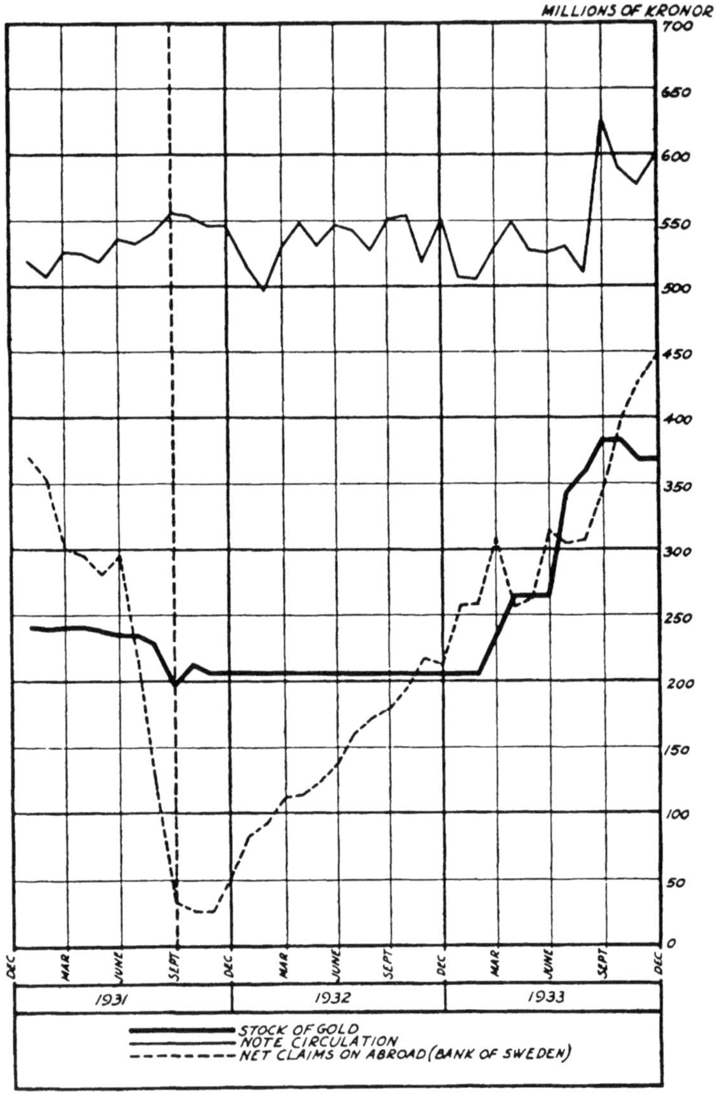

CHART 3. NOTE CIRCULATION, STOCK OF GOLD (IN GOLD KRONOR) AND NET CLAIMS ON ABROAD OF THE BANK OF SWEDEN.

Source: The Skandinaviska Kreditaktiebolaget.

CHART 4a. INDEXES OF WHOLESALE PRICES

1913 equal 100.

Source: The Svenska Handelsbanken and The Kommerskollegium.

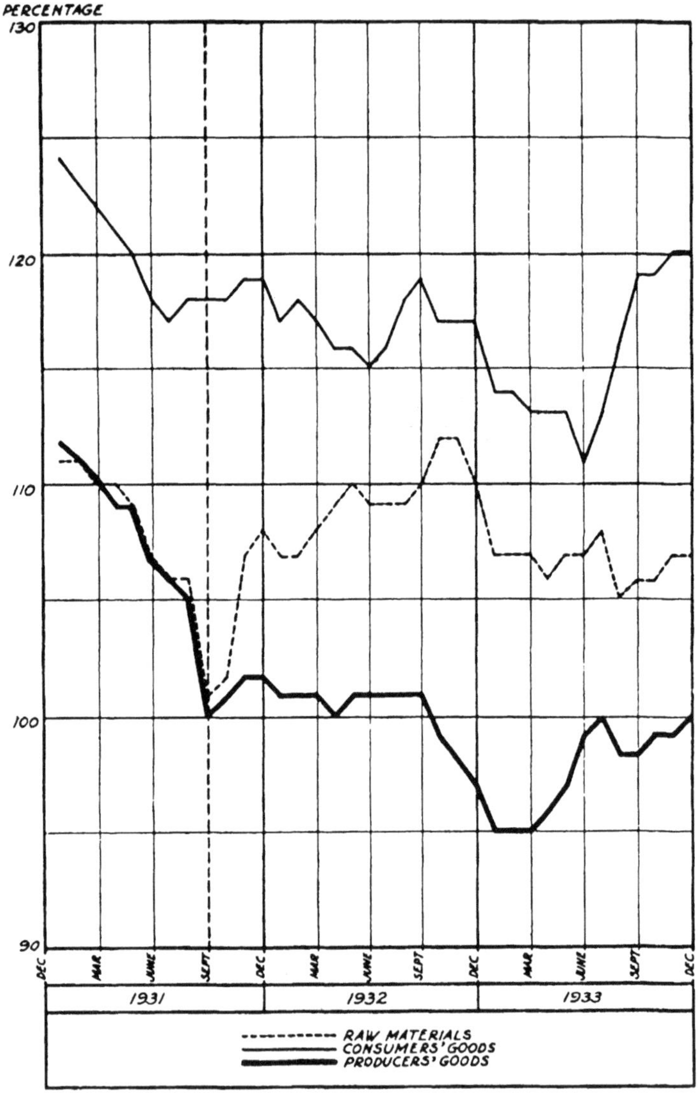

CHART 4b. INDEXES OF WHOLESALE PRICES

1913 equal 100.

Source: The Svenska Handelsbanken and The Kommerskollegium.

reach fulfillment. "Domestic goods" and "exported goods" continued their steady decline throughout the year, while "imported goods" rose rather sharply, particularly during the third quarter of the year. "Total producers' goods" also declined somewhat, while "consumers' goods," as indicated by the index of the Svenska Handelsbanken, remained more or less unaltered until the fourth quarter of

TABLE VIII[8]

CHANGES IN THE BANK OF SWEDEN INDEX DURING 1932

September 1931 = 100. (Weekly data)

January	99.9	July	101.7
	100.2		101.6
	101.1		101.4
	100.1		101.4
February	100.7		101.1
	100.8	August	100.9
	100.9		100.9
	101.0		100.8
March	101.1		100.6
	101.0	September	100.7
	101.0		100.6
	101.1		100.5
April	101.0		100.5
	101.1	October	100.4
	101.0		100.4
	100.9		100.5
	100.9		100.6
May	101.0		100.8
	101.1	November	101.0
	101.1		101.2
	101.1		101.2
June	101.2		101.3
	101.3	December	101.3
	101.4		101.3
	101.4		101.0
			100.9
			100.8

[8] Source: Bank of Sweden.

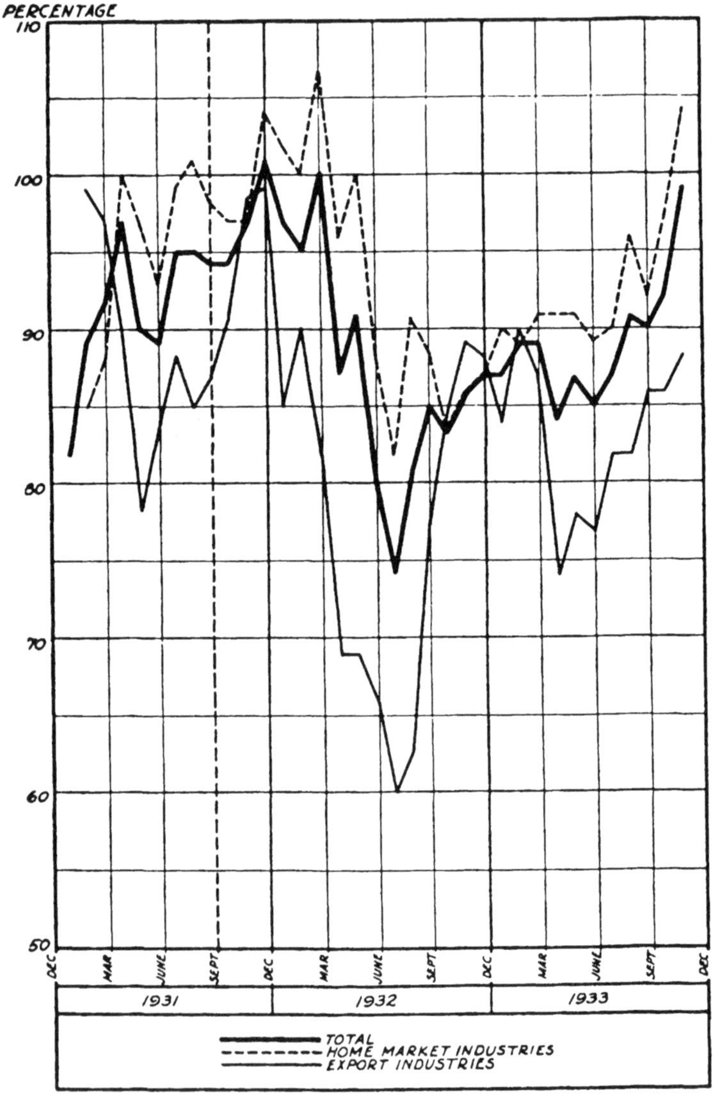

CHART 5. INDEXES OF PRODUCTION.

Adjusted for seasonal variations. Monthly averages 1925–1930 equal 100.

Source: The Kommerskollegium.

the year, when the index shows a sharp decline. The figures for "all goods," according to the data assembled by the Royal Board of Trade, show about the same trend as is shown by "consumers' goods." On the other hand the index for "raw materials" tends upwards throughout the year, until the beginning of November, when that also begins to decline. The index of the Bank of Sweden also remained steady, showing that the purchasing power of the krona in the hands of the general public had been maintained.[9]

Before considering the reasons for the failure of the price-raising program of the Bank of Sweden, it will, perhaps, be worth our while to consult the index of production prepared by the "Sveriges Industriförbund."[10]

From this diagram it may be seen that a considerable decline in production took place during the second quarter of the year. This is partly explained by the mounting obstacles to Swedish exports, which were raised by the aggravation of the world depression. A strike in the pulp industry, which lasted during the entire second quarter of the year, likewise contributed greatly to this decline. It is also well to remember that the Kreuger crisis of March, 1932, caused a temporary shock to confidence in Sweden's economic structure, both at home and abroad.

Not only the figures for production, but also those for railway traffic and the clearing of the

[9] See Table VIII.

[10] See Chart 5.

Bank of Sweden, indicate that the volume of trade at this time fell to a new low level. It should be noted, however, that several of the home market industries, favored by the rates of exchange, enjoyed comparatively good business. For example, the importation of wool, cotton, and rubber during the first two quarters of the year was larger than during the corresponding period of the preceding year; whereas, the importation of finished manufactures made from these products was greatly diminished. In the iron market also, the imports showed a much greater reduction than the exports.

Sweden did not, however, benefit greatly through the general rise in the prices of certain industrial raw products, as Sweden's principal export goods consist of requisites for production, which showed no rise in price during the period.[11]

The krona rate of exchange for the pound sterling remained virtually stable throughout the year, although there was a shift from a lower to a higher level after the Kreuger crisis; whereas, previous to the Kreuger debacle, the krona remained stable at about the old mint par. Following that collapse it was maintained at about 19.5 kr. to the pound until the last month of 1932, when the rate again began to approach mint parity.

SUMMARY OF RESULTS DURING 1932

The facts enumerated above show that the Bank of Sweden was not entirely successful in bringing about the desired results, particularly as wholesale

[11] Skandinaviska Kreditaktiebolaget, *Quarterly Reports*, 1932.

prices, instead of rising tended to decline. According to Professor Ohlin, the Kreuger crisis, and the general uncertainty in Swedish economic life resulting therefrom, made the psychological conditions unfavorable for a policy of credit expansion and price "reflation." There would nevertheless have been, in Professor Ohlin's opinion, a chance of bringing about a rise in the price level had the Bank of Sweden taken energetic measures (e. g., large bond purchases) and had such measures been supplemented by an increased demand for capital for public works.[12]

Subsequent information, however, points to the fact that the Bank of Sweden actually bought government securities during 1932, amounting to approximately two hundred million kronor. These purchases seem to have been intended, not as an energetic means of raising prices, but rather as an aid to the banking community after the downfall of the Kreuger concern.

Because of the hampering influence of the Kreuger crisis, the monetary policies of the Bank of Sweden encountered unusually unfavorable circumstances, which goes a long way towards explaining the failure of the price raising program. The commercial banks, which bettered their liquidity considerably, were in a position to lift the credit restrictions entirely; they were not, however, called upon to extend much credit to industry and trade. The diagram below also shows a sharp de-

[12] This opinion was brought forth in September, 1932. See B. Ohlin, "Sweden's Monetary Policy," in Svenska Handelsbanken, *Index*, Vol. VII, No. 81.

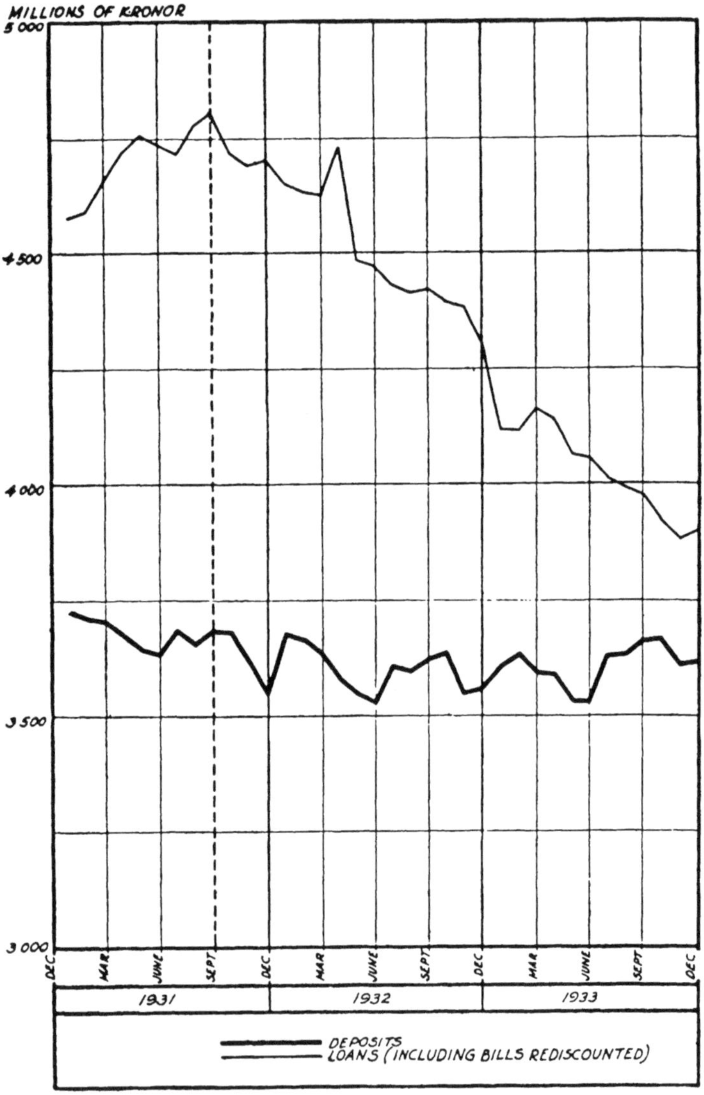

CHART 6. DEPOSITS AND LOANS (INCLUDING BILLS REDISCOUNTED), OF THE COMMERCIAL BANKS.

The data refers to end of each month.

Source: The Skandinaviska Kreditaktiebolaget.

cline, during the last nine months of the year, in the combined volume of loans and rediscounts.[13]

As a whole the program failed to attain the desired results in 1932. Although the purchasing power of the currency in the hands of the consumer was preserved, industrial production declined, and the labor market was disrupted. That the general price level remained relatively stable is no doubt largely to be explained by diverging price movements counteracting one another.

[13] See Chart 6.

CHAPTER VIII

The Second Revision of the Program

During the first quarter of 1933 general economic conditions did not differ materially from those prevailing during the last months of 1932. Unemployment remained at about the same level, and, at the beginning of March, 1933, it was estimated that between 180,000 and 190,000 persons were unable to find work.[1] The money market continued exceedingly easy, and loans and discounts by the commercial banks declined still further. The foreign exchange reserve of the Bank of Sweden showed that the Bank was in a very favorable position to influence the movements of the external value of the krona. The pound sterling fluctuated during January between 18.32 and 18.44; during February, however, the rate was permitted to go up to 18.90, as the pound during this month rose considerably in relation to the gold currencies. The dollar rate fluctuated during the first three months of 1933 between 5.40 and 5.545 kronor. Thus, Sweden enjoyed a fairly stable foreign exchange market with regard to both the pound and the gold currencies. Nevertheless domestic prices declined. This was particularly noticeable in the prices of agricultural commodities as well as in those of some leading export goods.

[1] See Chart 7.

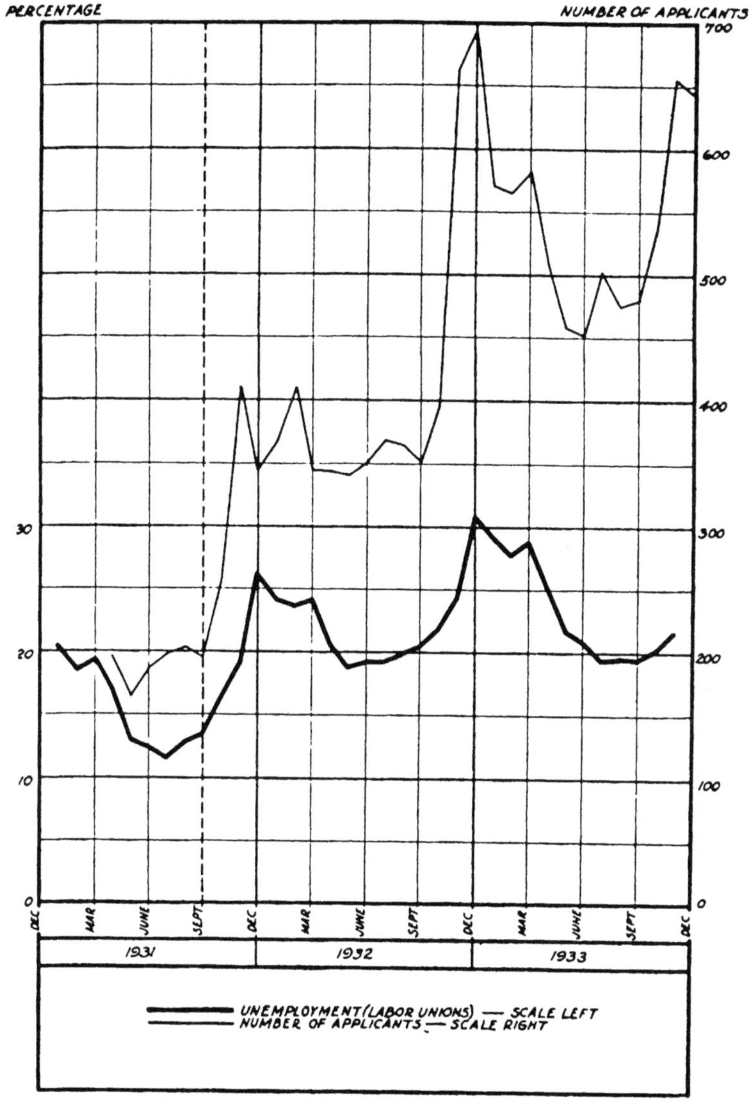

CHART 7. UNEMPLOYMENT IN THE LABOR UNIONS (IN PER CENT OF TOTAL NUMBER OF REGISTERED MEMBERS), AND NUMBER OF APPLICANTS PER HUNDRED VACANT POSITIONS DURING EACH MONTH.
Source: The Kommerskollegium.

Furthermore, no appreciable change in price trends and general economic conditions became noticeable during the second quarter of the year and the Crown called in an advisory committee to consider what should be done to further domestic production and to better conditions in the labor market.

This committee, made up of experts in political economy and of representatives of industry, agriculture, and banking, considered what should be done in the event of various probable developments abroad. If the leading nations should enter upon a program calculated to raise their domestic price levels, it was deemed advisable that Sweden should tie her currency to theirs. But, in the event that united world action was not undertaken, Sweden was advised to concentrate exclusively upon her domestic situation. This was to be done by continuing an *independent* monetary program with the ends in view of stopping the decline; if possible, gradually raising the wholesale price level; and, at the same time, maintaining the cost of living as stable as possible. No proposal was, however, advanced to force down the foreign value of the currency in order to obtain a temporary gain in exports. Such action, it was felt, would be of no lasting benefit, as it would merely aggravate the already chaotic conditions in the foreign exchange markets throughout the world.

The means to be used in bringing about a rise in the domestic level of prices were, according to one of the members of the Committee, Professor Gustav

Cassel, "alleviations in the bank rate and in the grant of credits." It was also proposed that the Bank of Sweden "should intervene *actively* for the stated purpose," by aiding in the financing of expenditures for unemployment relief.

The lack of an open market for short-term government obligations compelled such aid to be undertaken by having the Bank of Sweden rediscount, freely, such short-term Treasury bills as the government might issue for the financing of relief projects. The commercial banks which took up these bills on the market were thus enabled to pass them on to the central institution. This would make it possible for the commercial banks to transfer the burden to the Bank of Sweden and render them free to meet whatever increase there was in the demand for credit from trade and industry. It should be recognized, however, that the Bank of Sweden acts independently of the government, and that, therefore, no direct *demands* could be made on the Bank. The Bank, so the Committee observed, "should not be given any instructions in regard to monetary policy beyond those which are involved in defining the aim of that policy."

The coördination of the monetary policies of the Bank of Sweden and the public work projects is, of course, a sound principle. But as it happened that, because of continued strikes in the building industry, very few public works projects were started during the year (1933), the theory has not as yet received a fair test in practice.

During this period the Bank of Sweden also purchased gold, partly in the domestic market, and partly abroad, mainly in the United States and France. While the gold reserve of the Bank of Sweden was increased thereby, the value of the krona showed a tendency to decrease in relation to the gold currencies. This reduction in some instances facilitated Swedish exports.[2]

ECONOMIC DEVELOPMENTS DURING THE LATTER PART OF 1933

The general economic improvement, which was already noticeable during the second quarter, became increasingly pronounced during the ensuing months, although labor conflicts continued. The unemployment figures, adjusted for seasonal variations, showed a steady decline from 21.34 in March to an index number of 19.12 in September, when a further reduction took place so that in October the index number was 18.07. There is no doubt that this improvement, as reflected in growing export figures, was due to an increase in production and trade in a number of important industries. The excess of commodity imports during the period from January to August declined by 124 million kronor, as compared with the same period of the preceding year. However, the dispute that arose in the building industry in April is still (December, 1933) going on, and is responsible for a substantial rise in unemployment both in that industry and in others that are allied to it.[3]

[2] See Chart 3.

[3] "Economic Survey," Svenska Handelsbanken, *Index*, December, 1933. See Chart 8.

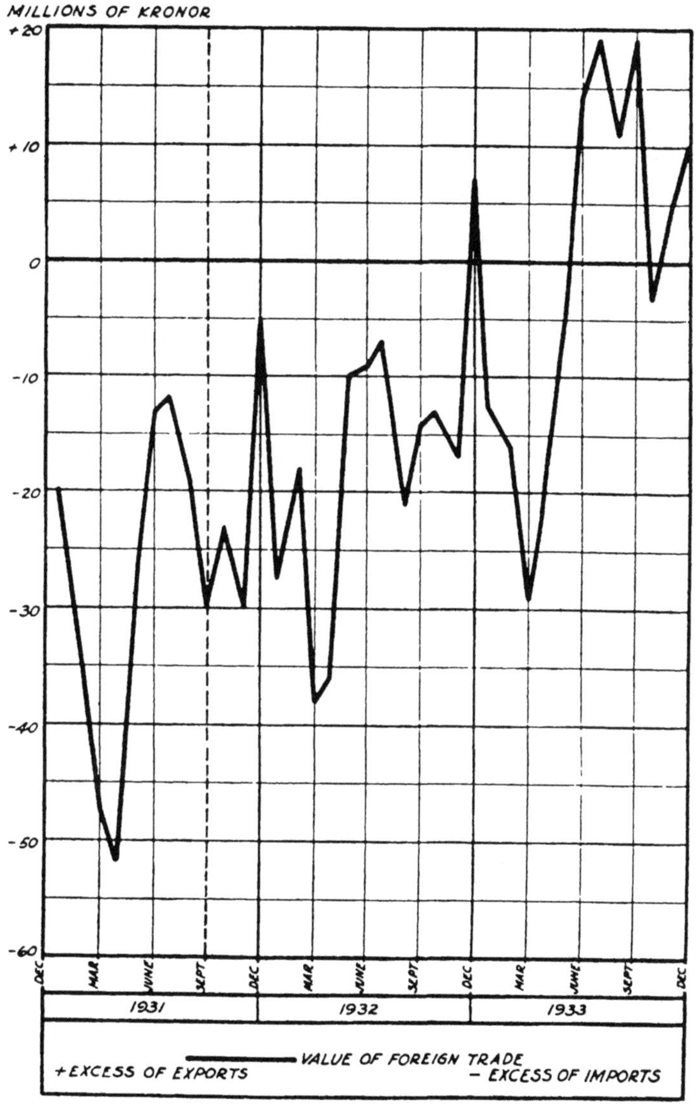

CHART 8. CHANGES IN THE BALANCE OF TRADE.
Source: The Skandinaviska Kreditaktiebolaget.

The data showing the value of Sweden's foreign trade appear continuously favorable during the fourth quarter. For the last three months of the year (1933) exports exceeded imports by 21 million kronor. The aggregate value for the first eleven months of 1933, however, shows an excess of imports over exports amounting to approximately 20 million kronor. On the other hand the surplus of imports during the same period of the preceding year was no less than 214.2 million kronor. The foreign trade position of Sweden has consequently improved greatly during this year, which may be attributed, to some extent, to greater industrial activity in Sweden's foreign markets. But it must not be overlooked that the Bank of Sweden has adhered to a policy of lowering the gold value of the Swedish currency, contrary to the advice of the committee of experts.[4]

The general trend of wholesale prices was definitely upward during the latter part of 1933. Most pronounced was the rise in "export goods" and "consumers' goods," while "raw materials" showed a tendency to weaken during November. "Imported goods" declined until April, when the index figure suddenly rose, only to steady down again. It should be noted, also, that with the exception of the prices for export and import goods, the indices have not to any appreciable extent surpassed their respective levels of September, 1931. It has, therefore, been impossible so far to bring about the desired rise in domestic wholesale prices

[4] Cf. Chart 2 and Appendix.

although, as pointed out above, the general trend during the last month of the year appears more hopeful than at any time during the experiment.

TABLE IX

MONTHLY INDEX OF THE BANK OF SWEDEN, 1933

September 1931 = 100

January	99,9	July	99,3
February	100,0	August	99,4
March	99,3	September	98,7
April	99,0	October	98,4
May	98,9	November	98,5
June	98,8	December	98,5

The money market is still characterized by a surplus of funds, which has led to a renewed reduction in interest rates. The rediscounting of the commercial banks has also dwindled until it is almost negligible. The gold reserve of the Bank of Sweden increased slightly during the last three months of the year 1933, while the foreign bill portfolio of the Bank rose sharply from 3 to 184 million kronor. During the same period the demand balances held by the Bank of Sweden with foreign banks declined by about 70 million kronor.[5]

The reason for the superabundance of money was to a great extent to be found in the practice of business enterprises of keeping a part of their working capital on current account with the commercial banks in expectation of a further upturn in business activity. An added reason for the ease of the money market was that both industrial enterprises and the commercial banks, endeavoring to protect

[5] See Chart 9.

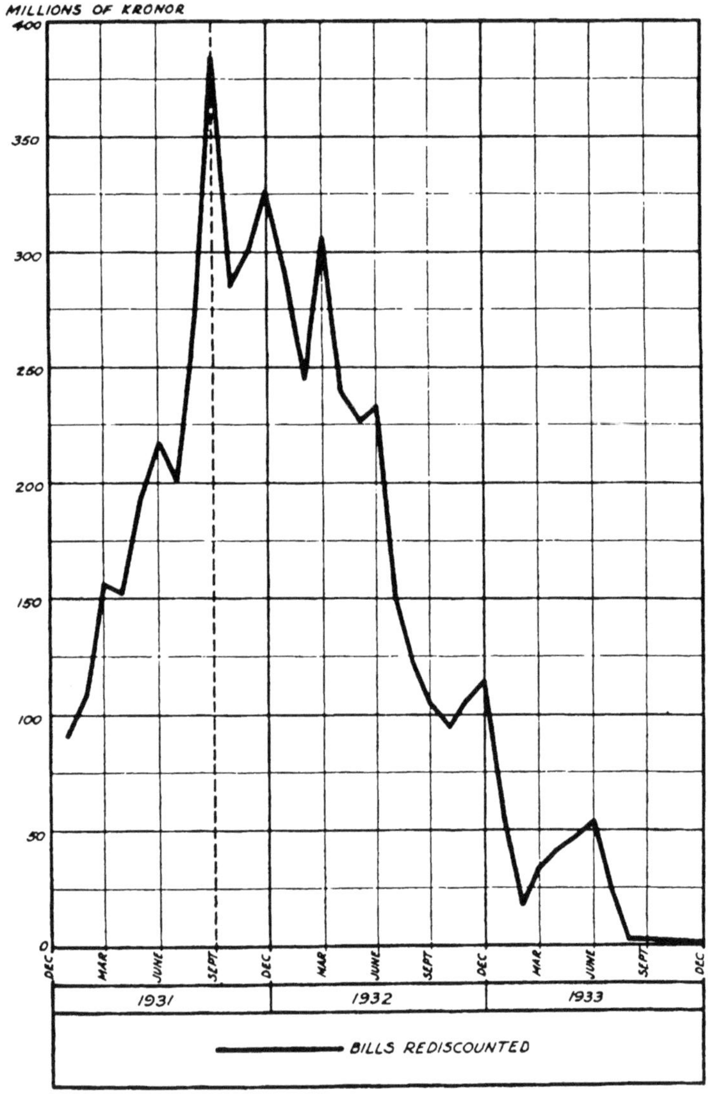

CHART 9. AMOUNT OF BILLS REDISCOUNTED BY THE COMMERCIAL BANKS.

The data refers to end of each month.

Source: The Skandinaviska Kreditaktiebolaget.

themselves against losses, sold a substantial part of their holdings of foreign exchange to the Bank of Sweden. The exceptionally easy conditions may best be portrayed by pointing out that the interest rate on long term deposits with the commercial banks was, on September 1, reduced to two and a half per cent, a record low in the history of Swedish banking. The trend of the krona in terms of pound sterling and French francs is illustrated on Chart 2. It is also worthy of note that, during the latter part of the year, some new industrial issues were placed on the bond market which, owing to the easy conditions in the money market and to falling interest rates, has been quite active during recent months, while the stock market has remained "dull and unsettled."

THE POSITION OF THE BANK OF SWEDEN

The favorable development of Sweden's foreign trade, as well as the excess of exports over imports of securities together with the Bank's policy of maintaining the external value of the krona in terms of pound sterling practically unchanged during the latter part of 1933 goes a long way toward explaining the favorable reserve position of the central institution. The total reserve of gold and foreign exchange,[6] which at the end of 1931 stood at 302 millions of kronor, increased in the following year to 462 millions of kronor and on December 31, 1933, the figure was no less than 763 millions of kronor.

[6] Inclusive of foreign exchange held in the commercial banks.

During 1933 the Bank of Sweden also operated at a profit of about 10.6 millions of kronor, *if* the value of the gold holding of the Bank is calculated on the price for gold in the open market in London on the last day of the year, and if the value of the foreign exchange portfolio is based on the foreign exchange quotations as of December 31, 1933. On the other hand the Bank has operated at a *loss* of approximately 100 millions of kronor if the gold holding is measured in terms of the statutory price for gold, and the reserve of foreign exchange in terms of the "old" parities. Obviously it is impossible to foretell either the probable profit or deficit of the Bank, until the krona is again stabilized in terms of gold and foreign currencies. The Bank is compelled to run the risk of operating at a loss, or else discontinue its efforts to improve the domestic price structure. Although the Banking Committee has been somewhat too optimistic as regards the efficacy of the monetary tools of the Bank of Sweden in achieving a rise in the wholesale price level, it is deemed advisable to continue the present policy in the hope that general economic conditions will soon give rise to an increased demand for credits for industrial purposes. It is also felt that the question of the profitableness of the operations of the central institution should not be permitted to interfere with the objective of raising wholesale prices independently of the trend of prices in foreign countries.

CHAPTER IX

Summary and Conclusions

Sweden's monetary program, which has been in operation since the last week in September, 1931, is essentially an emergency measure, having for its ultimate objective the mitigation of the economic depression. The program may be subdivided into the following three parts: (1) efforts to prevent inflation of currency and credit; (2) preservation of the internal purchasing power of the krona in the hands of the general public; (3) a gradual rise in wholesale prices as a means of stimulating domestic production.

These objectives may be summarized under one heading—an independent regulation of prices by means of monetary tools.

The responsibility of carrying out the program is placed with the Bank of Sweden, which acts independently of the government, although it is a "Bank of Parliament."

The measures used by the Bank of Sweden are as follows: (1) changes in the official bank rate; (2) transactions in the foreign exchange market; (3) buying and selling of gold both at home and abroad; (4) purchases of government bonds.

The extent of the efforts of the Bank may best be realized by enumerating these facts: the official bank rate, which, in the latter part of September,

1931, was raised from six to eight per cent, has since then been lowered gradually until it was in December, 1933, 2½ per cent. The purchases of gold, foreign exchange, and government securities total approximately 950 million kronor, or about 400 million kronor more than the average volume of money in circulation during the last 27 months.

The following results have been obtained: (1) the process of deflation has been halted; (2) the danger of currency and credit inflation was averted; (3) the internal purchasing power of the krona has been maintained reasonably well; (4) a gradual rise of the wholesale price level has not taken place.

COMMENTS

1. In considering the objectives, the following observation should be made: the program was inaugurated during a period of severe economic depression, and furthermore, the depression had then run for more than 18 months.

It should also be noted that the efforts of the Bank of Sweden to regulate prices occurred during a period when the price structure was highly distorted by the vicious spiral of deflation. Wholesale prices had declined much more than retail prices, while wages (nominal) were entirely "out of line" with wholesale prices.

2. As regards the policy of the Bank of Sweden, it should be noted that its transactions in the foreign exchange market had a two-fold aim, of which the first was to maintain the krona as stable as possible in terms of the pound sterling, without

"pegging" it to the British currency. During certain periods, however, the krona has actually been "pegged" to the pound. This has been done temporarily, and as an expedient, not as a policy in itself. Secondly, the krona has been depreciated in terms of the gold currencies.[1] The object of this two-fold policy has been to prevent, as far as possible, a decline in import and export prices, as a means of escape from a further deflation of the domestic price structure.

The government bond purchases were undertaken, mainly, in order to strengthen the banking community after the Kreuger crisis.

3. In reviewing the *results* of the program it should be realized that, although it has been impossible to achieve a slow rise of the domestic wholesale price level, the Swedish wholesale prices have not fallen as low as have corresponding prices in some other countries not having a definite monetary program.

The index of the Bank of Sweden remained virtually unchanged for more than fifteen months, while during the remaining months, for which the data is available at the time of writing, the index receded gradually to about 98 per cent of its norm.

The unfavorable circumstances mentioned in the two preceding chapters no doubt go a long way towards explaining the fluctuations in the index of production. However, it is noteworthy that the index of production begins to move upwards after the severe setback following the Kreuger crisis in

[1] See Appendix.

the spring of 1932, several months before the upward movement began in domestic as well as export prices. This may partly be accounted for by a growing demand for Swedish goods in the foreign markets.

It is also a noteworthy fact that unemployment grew steadily worse for more than a year of "managed currency"; since then, however, the statistics show a gradual but slow improvement. Wages are still "out of line" with the price structure as a whole. True, they have been reduced somewhat, but not nearly enough to correspond to the trends of prices.

The maladjustments in the price structure have been smoothed out slightly. The reason for this better balance is, not, however, to be traced to the policy of the Bank of Sweden; wholesale prices have not risen to meet wages and retail prices—rather, the contrary has occurred.

During the last few months of 1933 Sweden enjoyed an upswing in prices and business activity. This enjoyment, however, Sweden shares with most other countries, as there has been a gradual improvement in the general world economic outlook since the spring of 1933.

CONCLUSIONS

Owing to a variety of circumstances which strongly influenced the developments in Sweden during this period, it is quite impossible to state to what extent the policies of the Bank of Sweden have actually been instrumental in bringing about the developments herein summarized. However, I venture to draw the following conclusions:

The Bank of Sweden, in coöperation with the commercial banks, succeeded in averting currency and credit inflation during the early part of the program.

All efforts to expand credit on the domestic market have failed. Sweden has consequently experienced the same difficulties as did the Federal Reserve System when it attempted to "pump out" credit by means of operations in the government bond market. The experiences of Sweden and America seem to prove, therefore, that credit cannot be "pumped out," and that a demand for credit must exist on the part of the business community before the banks are in a position to lend.

A lowering of the official bank rate, accompanied by a decline in interest and discount rates, merely eased the money market but did not initiate credit expansion; while, to some extent, it stimulated the bond market.

On the purely domestic market, the policies of the Bank of Sweden have not been particularly successful. The stability of retail, and, to some extent, wholesale prices are largely the result of diverging price movements offsetting one another. This stability, does not, however, signify that there is a balance in the price structure as a whole.

The transactions in the foreign exchange market (buying and selling of foreign exchange as well as purchases of gold) have been more successful in influencing the trends of prices than has the changes in the official bank rate.

Although there can be no doubt that the Bank of Sweden has done much to avert an aggravation of the depression by controlling the external value of the krona, still the movements of export and import prices have largely been determined by price developments abroad. The transactions in the foreign exchange market have served mainly as a means to prevent a further lowering of the price structure.

The monetary program has not been an adequate means to lift the country out of the grip of the depression.

As a preventive economic factor the monetary policy has, however, been reasonably sufficient.

There can be no doubt, that the formulation of a *definite objective* for the policy has served to maintain confidence in the future value of the krona.

THE OUTLOOK FOR THE FUTURE

In the event that the large nations return to gold and establish a truly international gold standard, Sweden will follow their example. Sweden is a creditor nation; she has again an excess of exports over imports of commodities; and furthermore, the Bank of Sweden possesses a substantial reserve of gold. Sweden is, therefore, in a position to coöperate with the leading nations in the rehabilitation of the international monetary machinery.

Of immediate importance to Sweden, is, however, the trend of prices in her export and import markets. At present this trend is upwards, indicating that the upswing in business activity, which has been noticeable for the last few months, might well be sustained. Whether the improvement can be further accelerated is, of course, entirely a matter of conjecture.

Appendix

Although no effort has been made to interpret the Swedish monetary program in the light of economic theory, the analysis given would not be nearly complete without some further observations.

The program is significant for one particular reason: that it is, probably, the first time in history that a nation has suspended a monetary standard and followed such an action by establishing a new and *independent standard.*

The determination of this standard has been, largely, the index of the central institution. According to the statistics appearing in the text, this index has, so far, remained virtually unchanged. This is partly because the index as presented is not adjusted for: e.g., increase in taxation. Such an adjustment has been made by Professor Ohlin, and he arrives at the conclusion that in 1933 the index declined approximately 3.6 per cent, as against 2 per cent in the index herein utilized.

By and large the commercial banks have adjusted their discount and interest rates so as to conform with the changes made in the rediscount rate. This does not, however, hold true of the provincial offices of the large commercial banks. With rising bond prices, the savings banks, which have comparatively low managerial expense, have found it profitable to maintain their interest rates relatively high, as a means of attracting funds from the public, both directly, and indirectly through the transfers of savings accounts from the commercial banks to the savings banks. Some provincial offices of commercial banks have, therefore, been fearful about adjusting their rates to a level below the one of the savings banks. Through negotiations, a satisfactory uniformity in rates has now (January, 1934) been achieved, and negotiations are being carried on for a further lowering of the rate structure.

The decline of loans (including rediscounting) cannot serve as an adequate measure of the *demand* for commercial loans; as the commercial banks, because of the desire to preserve and improve their liquidity, have been reluctant to grant credits. In coöperation with the commercial banks, the government began, in the early part of 1934, an investigation into the advisability of establishing a government-controlled credit institution to care for the need of comparatively long-term credits on the part of small and average-sized enterprises: particularly as, through changes in the Bank Act (1933), the commercial banks are compelled to diminish their long-term (renewals) loans. It is the object of the government to do whatever it can to facilitate commercial and industrial borrowings by worthy enterprises that under existing conditions cannot be amply supplied with credit for an economically sound expansion. It is also proposed that the new institution shall grant comparatively long-term credits to export industries. The need for maintaining the credit standing of the Swedish government and the liquidity of the commercial banks is well recognized, and no pressure is being brought on the commercial banks to lower their credit standards.

During the early part of the program the Bank of Sweden faced the difficulty of *obtaining* foreign exchange for purposes of relieving the domestic price structure from the pressure of declining prices abroad. During 1933, however, the Bank has been face to face with the problem of investing its exceptionally large reserve of foreign exchange.

In its search for foreign exchange, the Bank was aided by the circumstance, which to some extent was brought about by the Bank's own policy, of Swedish citizens disposing of their holdings of foreign securities. The excess of exports over imports of securities during 1932 amounted, roughly, to 115 millions of kronor, and during the first nine months of 1933, for which data is available at the time of writing (January, 1934), the excess measured 65 millions of kronor as compared to 72 millions during the corresponding period of 1932. On several occasions the Bank, also, adjusted its rates for the krona, particularly in terms of the pound sterling, so as to induce the holders of foreign exchange to sell their claims to the Bank. It may also be pointed out that Swedish exporters obtained foreign exchange credits at times in large volume in foreign money centers, as a means of minimizing their own exchange risks. It is not known to the writer, however, to just what extent the Bank of Sweden benefited by such credits.

Actual disturbances on the international currency market, as, e.g., the banking holiday in the United States, as well as fear of the coming of such disturbances, have at times served as determining circumstances in the Bank's foreign exchange policy. An analysis of such occurrences leads, however, to the conclusion that although the Bank at times deviated somewhat from its immediate aim of achieving stability of the domestic price structure, the ultimate results of such deviations tended to facilitate the stability.

The chart below shows the movements of wholesale prices in Great Britain, France and Sweden. Each line indicates the deviation, in per cent, as of September, 1931. It is quite noticeable that in Sweden wholesale prices have deviated less than is the case both in Great Britain and in France.

In this connection, the reader will do well to consult also the chart showing changes in the external value of the krona in terms of the pound sterling and the French franc. The "offsetting" influence of the Bank's foreign exchange policy is then quite noticeable.

The gold purchases which have been made both at home (Boliden Gold Mines) and abroad have tended to lower the krona in terms of the "gold currencies." In so far as such purchases have been intended as a means to diminish the "gold value" of the krona, the Bank has followed a policy of depreciation of the krona, contrary to the advice of the Committee of Experts (Spring, 1933). The main purpose of the gold buying program, however, has

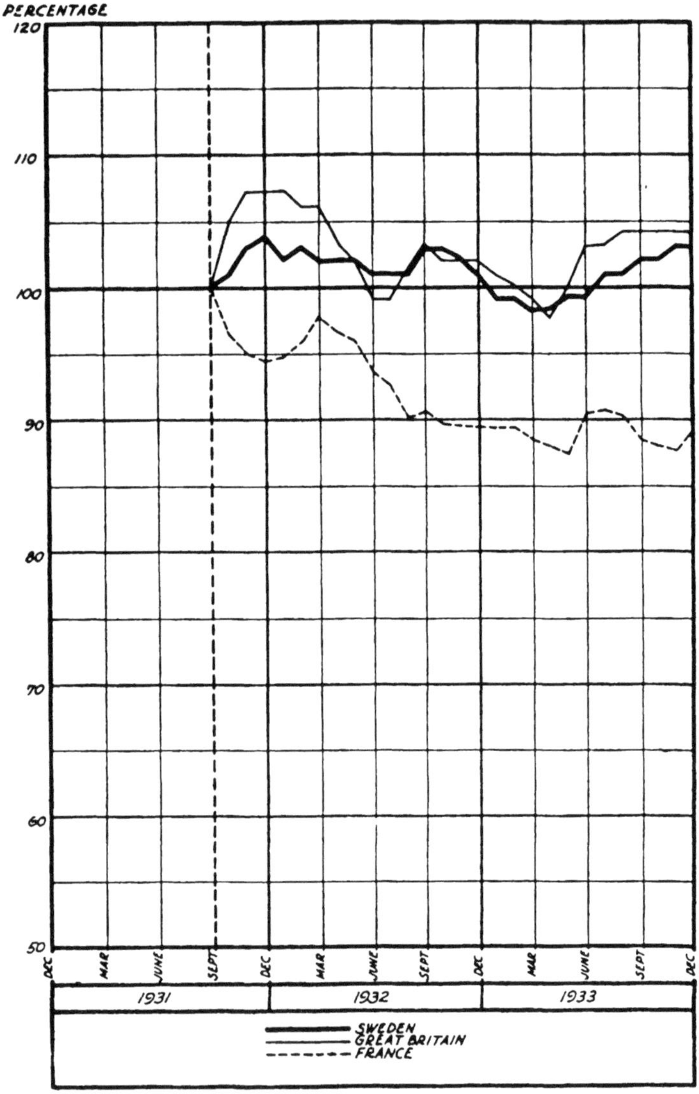

CHART 10. CHANGES IN THE WHOLESALE PRICE LEVELS IN GREAT BRITAIN, FRANCE AND SWEDEN.

September 1931 equals 100.

Source: The Kommerskollegium. (Great Britain: Board of Trade), (France: Statist. Générale) (Sweden: Kommerskollegium).

been to minimize the risk involved in the foreign exchange reserve by investing part of the foreign claims in gold, which the bank had earmarked for its account with foreign banks, while some of the gold was also transferred to the vaults of the Bank of Sweden. The rising price for gold on the international market undoubtedly played an important rôle in these transactions. All transactions in gold were made during 1933. The Bank purchased a total amount of 159 millions of kronor of gold and sold 13 millions. The sales took place during October and November.

Bibliography

Anderson, Benjamin M., Jr., "On The Practical Impossibility of a Commodity Dollar. *The Chase Economic Bulletin*. Vol. XIII. No. 4. (December 13, 1933.)

Bankoutskottets memorial, No. 1, Stockholm, 1932, 1933, 1934.

Cassel, Gustav, "Sveriges Valutapolitik." Skandinaviska Kreditaktiebolaget, *Quarterly Report*. July, 1933.

Davidson, David, *Felet i Sveriges Valutapolitik*, Almqvist & Wiksell, Upsala, 1932.

Fisher, Irving, *Inflation?* The Adelphi Company, New York, May, 1933.

Heckscher, Eli F., *Sveriges Penningpolitik*, P. A. Norstedt & Söner, Stockholm, November, 1931.

Kock, Karin, *A Study of Interest Rates*, P. S. King and Son, Ltd., London, November, 1928.

Kommerskollegium, *Kommersiella Meddelanden*, Stockholm, 1931, 1932, 1933.

Midland Bank, *Monthly Review*, London, October-November, 1932.

Myrdal, Gunnar, *Sveriges väg genom penningkrisen*, Natur och Kultur, Stockholm, November, 1931.

Ohlin, Bertil, "Sweden's Monetary Policy," *Index*, Vol. VII, No. 81 (September, 1932).

———, "The Inadequacy of Price Stabilization," *Index*, Vol. VIII, No. 96 (December, 1933).

Skandinaviska Kreditaktiebolaget, *Quarterly Report*, Stockholm 1931, 1932, 1933.

Svenska Handelsbanken, *Index*, Stockholm, 1931, 1932, 1933.

Willis, H. P., and B. H. Beckhart, *Foreign Banking Systems*, Henry Holt & Company, New York, 1929.

Index

Bei Fragen zur Produktsicherheit wenden Sie sich bitte an:
If you have any questions regarding product safety,
please contact:

Walter de Gruyter GmbH
Genthiner Straße 13
10785 Berlin
productsafety@degruyterbrill.com